COMMITTEE ON HISTORIC ARCHITECTURE OF THE MUNICIPAL ART SOCIETY OF NEW YORK

 THE following members of the Municipal Art Society have served on the Committee on Historic Architecture, which was initiated by Edward Steese in 1951. This Committee has reviewed hundreds of structures in Greater New York, between the years 1951 and 1963, to determine which should be included in the Index of Architecturally Notable Structures. It deserves all credit for this work and for the assistance given to the New York Chapter of the American Institute of Architects in documenting buildings for the files of the Historic American Buildings Survey of the National Park Service.

CHAIRMEN

Daniel M. C. Hopping　1960 —　　　　　Edward Steese　1955–1956
Alan Burnham　1958–1960　　　　　　　Agnes A. Gilchrist　1953–1955
Walter Knight Sturges　1956–1958　　　　Edward Steese　1951–1953

HONORARY MEMBERS

Talbot F. Hamlin (deceased)　　　　　　James Grote Van Derpool

COMMITTEE MEMBERS

Wayne Andrews　　　　　　　　　　Raphael Hume (dec'd.)　　　　　Samuel W. Patterson
Mrs. Richard H. Dana　　　　　　　William N. Jayme　　　　　　　Powell Pierpoint
Mrs. Byron Dexter　　　　　　　　Oliver B. Jennings　　　　　　　Henry Hope Reed, Jr.
Miss Maud E. Dilliard　　　　　　　Francis Keally　　　　　　　　Francis W. Roudebush
Kenneth H. Dunshee　　　　　　　Theodore Koch　　　　　　　　William H. Russell (dec'd.)
Mrs. Maximilian Elser, Jr. (dec'd.)　L. Bancel LaFarge　　　　　　Whitney North Seymour
Brendan Gill　　　　　　　　　　Charles Magruder (dec'd.)　　　J. Sanford Shanley
Harmon H. Goldstone　　　　　　Loring McMillen　　　　　　　Daniel D. Streeter
Arthur C. Holden　　　　　　　　John E. Nicholson (dec'd.)　　　Edgar I. Williams

NEW YORK LANDMARKS

NEW YORK

A STUDY & INDEX OF
ARCHITECTURALLY NOTABLE STRUCTURES
IN GREATER NEW YORK

LANDMARKS

EDITED BY ALAN BURNHAM, A. I. A.

Published Under the Auspices of The Municipal Art Society of New York

by the Wesleyan University Press

MIDDLETOWN, CONNECTICUT

TO EDWARD STEESE

CONTENTS

LIST OF ILLUSTRATIONS

PICTURES IN TEXT

PLATES

NOTE: *The architecturally notable structures depicted here are arranged, borough by borough, chronologically by date of erection.*

Manhattan

Brooklyn

FOREWORD

WE New Yorkers tend to feel toward our city something like the mixture of love and hatred that Joyce must have felt toward his country the day he described it as the old sow that eats her farrow. This great, rebuffing, untender conurbation (and who that was wise would love a conurbation?) — how readily we lay claim to possessing it and how we long for some sign of its wishing to possess us in return! Yet no less readily, in the diesel stench of a midsummer afternoon, with the temperature well above a hundred, or in the unsniffable wind of a winter morning, with the temperature well below zero, we damn it as unfit for human habitation. And to render our emotions all the more unstable, we can never be sure from one moment to the next precisely what it is that we love or hate; if the city is a bride, then the honeymoon is exceedingly bizarre, because the face one wakes beside is rarely the face that one kissed goodnight.

This precariousness of identity has been, of course, a particular bane of the years since the Second World War. More and more, haven't we all been of two minds about the way New York has persisted in transforming itself — not, as in the old joke, by taking in the streets at night but by taking down the blocks by day? We've complained that the building boom has led this impetuous city to change its appearance too fast and too capriciously, and our sorrow at seeing precious landmarks beaten into rubble and carted off to the Jersey Meadows has canceled much of our pleasure in the glass towers that have leapt up, shining and aghast, in their place. (Some of us have even managed to regret that our seedy old friend Third Avenue, laddered with "L" shadows and reeking of stale beer, should have been turned so quickly and easily into the dapper arriviste it is today.) Lately, though, I've begun to wonder whether our mourning over these drastic urban changes isn't, like most mourning, self-indulgent. No sooner does the local boom threaten to subside than I find any number of reasons for admiring it. The faintest hint of things' coming to a standstill in this tirelessly tearing-down-and-building-up city — of a day when not a single workman between the Battery and Spuyten Duyvil would be digging, blasting, laying bricks, or welding — makes my heart sink. Maybe it will turn out that we don't want the city to stop making itself over, after all; that its incessant changingness isn't merely the source of its life but the secret of its charm.

Nevertheless, to hail the city in its newness (how it gleams by day! how it glows by night!) isn't to forget that it grows steadily, blessedly more ancient. New York is immortally young, but it has stairs that creak and stone gutters worn to the smoothness of a wheel rut in Pompeii. Surely it's the duty of true lovers of the city to seek out and cherish and try to preserve from the ravages of natural decay and commercial cupidity the best of the gifts that each succeeding boom has bestowed upon it. Let the wrecking ball of the present tumble the mediocrities of the past, as the wrecking ball of the future will tumble ours (which the unwary among us like to assume are the worst mediocrities of all time. Tut, tut! Little in the nineteen-sixties is apt to surpass in stultifying dullness those uncountable blocks of cheap, speculator-built, nineteenth-century brownstones.) Faceless nonentities of brick and stone may be swept aside; at the same time, we must fight hard to keep the wreckers' hands off what we believe, without false sentiment, deserves to be saved. The first step in such a battle is to know precisely what it is we're fighting for. Which are the buildings worthy of our interest and protection? If only a fraction of a given whole can be preserved, which fraction shall it be? Age alone is a poor test; piety is a worse. We care a little that this is a building in which Grandma slept; we care more that it is one in which — though not with Grandma — Washington slept; but at bottom our feeling is for the building and not the sleepers.

To identify our landmarks and to call expert attention to their distinguishing characteristics, here is this book. Thanks to Alan Burnham, the scholarly proprietor of the American Architectural Archive, and to the Municipal Art Society, which has been carrying on a not always requited love affair with New York for upward of three-quarters of a century, we have at last the necessary means of knowing where we stand. I find it hard to imagine that anyone who lives in New York can fail to become its passionate devotee — if you don't like it here, I think coarsely, why don't you go back to where you came from? I find it equally hard to imagine that any such devotee will be content to do without a book that is a veritable Kama Sutra, or manual of instruction, in the wooing of this incomparable city.

BRENDAN GILL

NEW YORK LANDMARKS

INTRODUCTION

OR MORE than seventy years the Municipal Art Society has dedicated its efforts to making New York City a more handsome and more humane environment in which to live and to work. The Society is interested in conserving the best of the past, in giving recognition to the best of the present, and in encouraging the best possible planning for the future. To this end, since its founding in 1892 by a group of young architects led by Richard Morris Hunt, it has promoted the highest standards for architecture, planning, landscape architecture, and preservation in the city's five boroughs.

In order to accomplish these objectives, the Society's membership, through service on its Board of Directors and its working committees, has contributed to many programs which have assisted in improving the city's welfare and beauty.

In the interests not only of conserving the city's distinguished architectural past but of making its pleasures a living part of the present, the Society has developed two programs for its members. The first is a complete and documented index of architecturally noteworthy buildings in Greater New York. This index was completed and published in 1957, in a mimeographed edition of some forty pages, under the title *New York Landmarks* — which, with certain corrections and additions, was reprinted three times. The present volume contains the latest revision of the index and is thus in a sense the fifth edition of *New York Landmarks;* but in most of its features — Brendan Gill's Foreword and the editor's explanatory chapters, the bibliography, and above all the photographs with their legends and placement maps — this book is entirely new. The original *New York Landmarks* has been used by the Landmarks Preservation Commission of the City of New York as a basis for its own program.

A second program devoted to stimulating interest in New York's past and present is a series of guided *Walking Tours,* which have proved extremely popular, through distinctive neighborhoods such as Gramercy Park, Wall Street, Greenwich Village, Brooklyn Heights, and Staten Island. These tours are concerned only with the most notable architecture of the city, past and present, including the modern architecture of mid-Manhattan, various aspects of town planning, and the best examples of landscape architecture in our parks.

One of the programs of the Society that has attracted considerable notice, because it has figured so prominently in the interest of the public, has been the plan for planting trees along city streets. A booklet, *It Grows on You,* which describes this activity, is distributed every year by the Society to architects, builders, property owners, city residents, and business firms and has produced tangible results.

The awards given each year by the Society, for distinguished public service and artistic achievement that have in some new way graced and beautified the city, have recognized important modern structures, distinguished examples of conservation, landscape architecture, and urban design.

The Municipal Art Society stands as the one organization in New York through which the layman and the businessman may join with the professional, with the sole purpose of enhancing the visual beauty of the city. There is no more vital function of the Society than the role played by its committees on city planning, zoning, landscape architecture, and civic action. They continue to guide public and official opinion on legislation affecting the Society's objectives. A close liaison with other civic organizations is maintained on these matters.

The committees of the Society implement its varied activities. It was the work of one of these, the Committee on Historic Architecture, that laid the groundwork upon which this book has been built. Many years of appraisal, selection, rejection, and addition of New York architecture by committee members resulted in the creation of the Index of Architecturally Notable Structures in Greater New York.

As the work of the Committee on Historic Architecture proceeded toward its first goal, assisting the New York Chapter of the American Institute of Architects to prepare a documented list of buildings in New York, for the Historic American Buildings Survey of the National Park Service, the idea of preparing the Index was formulated. This was the genesis of the mimeographed edition of *New York Landmarks.*

Later, when the work of the Committee was fairly well advanced, the New York Community Trust, through the interest of Ralph Hayes, made a financial contribution to the Society to extend the scope of its researches. This gift was intended to enable the Community Trust to inaugurate a program of placing metal plaques on architecturally noteworthy buildings throughout the city. It gave impetus to the whole study, resulting in many additions to the Index. This index of buildings was unique, in that it not only gave all the pertinent information about each building, but grouped them in categories of relative importance. These categories were intended to assist anyone interested to evaluate the relative merits of buildings.

Among problems facing the Committee on Historic Architecture were those encountered in performing the actual research relative to the buildings selected for inclusion. In the Index, we find first the name of the building or its owner. This was usually easy to establish. Addresses were obtained by field trips to the sites. Where a building was located on a corner site, we preferred to designate its location relative to such corner instead of giving the street number, as street numbers may change. A clearly designated corner location will usually be identifiable for generations, even after the building itself is gone. In giving these locations, the assumption was that one was standing in the center of the crossing, looking toward the building at the northwest corner or the southwest corner, etc., just as the points of a compass would indicate the direction of the corners, were it placed in the center of the intersection.

To find the name of the architect of a given building often involved considerable research. If, after checking the standard architectural works relating to New York (see Bibliography — Architects) no architect could be found, it was often necessary to take a field trip to check with the owners. Where the owners did not know, it then became necessary to check the newspapers for articles relative to the completion of the building with the hope that the architect's name would be given. New York City Building Department files were also consulted.

The dating of buildings was by far the most difficult task facing the Committee. In many cases only one date is given in the Index. Where this date could not be accurately established it is preceded by a "c," implying that it was built at about ("circa") that time. The complexities entailed in dating buildings could involve us in a lengthy discussion regarding methods of research. A simple explanation of what was done in this Index reveals the fact that one date represents the year the building was built, whereas two dates represent the year in which construction was begun and the year in which it was completed.

Many different words are used to indicate the commencement of construction, such as "begun," "commenced," "laying of cornerstone," etc.; while completion can include "completed," "dedicated," and, in the case of churches, "consecrated," etc. Between these dates several months or years may intervene; consequently, it is difficult to decide which are the appropriate dates to use.* Stylistically speaking, the date at which a building was designed is the most important, since construction might be delayed for as much as a year or more from the time at which it was designed, the plans remaining unchanged. Should there be a further delay during construction, or a time lag before the certificate of occupancy ("C.O.") was actually issued, further confusion might result. Such a building, judged by its style or appearance, might seem to be of an earlier date than was actually the case.

As to the attribution of styles, this usually required a field trip to make possible a careful analysis of the building's physical appearance, noting materials, type of plan, and ornament employed. The significance of the date was an additional factor which could contribute to the proper evaluation.

The Code to Special Features includes references which were added to highlight outstanding features in buildings, such as unusual or outstanding ironwork, mosaics, stained glass, or other features.

Due to the fact that there was such a wealth of material to be covered, the year 1930 was established as the terminal date of the Index. Two publications, *New York Architec-*

* H. V. Molesworth Roberts, "Recording Dates of Buildings." *Journal of the Society of Architectural Historians*, Vol. 12, No. 3, October 1953.

ture, 1650–1952, by Huson Jackson, and *Four Walking Tours of Modern Architecture in New York City*, by Ada Louise Huxtable, contribute to rounding out the period from 1930 to the present. A review of the Sunday *New York Times Magazine* will yield many interesting articles on buildings and an intelligent critical analysis of contemporary architecture.

The Index of Architecturally Notable Structures in Greater New York may be described as a skeleton of bare facts, upon which we can form only a preliminary estimate of what any given building might be like. The best resource we have is to visit the building itself, so that we can see it in three dimensions. Photographs will give us a good two-dimensional preview, but here we lack the ever changing impression which is obtained from walking around a building — the colors, the textures, and that elusive thing, the essence of architecture, that quality which reality alone can give, wherein the building almost speaks for itself, telling us of its great age or of its newness and of the times and influences which produced it.

Before presenting the Index and the accompanying materials, which represent the work of so many Society members and friends, the editor wishes to thank all of those who assisted the Committee on Landmarks. Perhaps the fact that this book exists at all should be credited to our president, Morris Ketchum, and his predecessors Harmon Goldstone and George Fitch, who have been my harshest critics. Their criticism stemmed only from their vital interest in *New York Landmarks* and their desire to see it completed.

The man who, more than any other, prepared the groundwork which made this book possible, who formed the committees and infected those who worked on them with his own enthusiasm, and who realized the importance of establishing sound categories, is Edward Steese, an architect, whose ability to design made him a true critic of buildings.

For encouragement at all stages of the work and for his friendly yet penetrating criticisms in architectural matters, drawn from his own considerable background of knowledge, I must thank Walter Knight Sturges, who preceded me as chairman of the Committee on Historic Architecture; and Daniel M. C. Hopping, who succeeded me, for his cooperation in expediting everything pertaining to this book.

No work of any magnitude could ever be undertaken in the Municipal Art Society without consulting Irene V. Walsh, Executive Secretary, who first came to the Society in 1912, and who alone had that continuity of knowledge pertaining to our goals which has always made the Society's work consistent and effective. Her successor, Jane Henderson, has been most cooperative in all phases of our work.

The Landmarks Preservation Commission, headed by Geoffrey Platt, has offered us every possible assistance and is vitally interested in *New York Landmarks* as an initial compendium from which it will begin its extensive labors, branching out to discover many new landmarks in all five boroughs.

Several gifts to the Society have contributed, directly or indirectly, to our endeavor. Among these were two contributions made to the Committee on Historic Architecture: one, for research, from Mrs. Richard Dana; and the other from the New York Community Trust, in connection with Ralph Hayes' program for erecting plaques on architecturally noteworthy buildings.

Charles E. Merrill contributed money to the Society for the publication of a book. This generous gift has been applied, in part, toward the preparation of *New York Landmarks*.

The most notable aid to the researches which were required to produce this book was a handsome loan proffered to the Society by Mr. Gregory Smith, a board member, on the condition that the Society should match his loan. This was all accomplished at one board meeting and, in effect, launched our activities.

A benefit held by Lord & Taylor in 1962, honoring the Municipal Art Society, resulted in funds to be used for the restoration of the Bethesda Fountain in Central Park and some additional funds which made possible a reduction in price for the first edition of *New York Landmarks*, putting it within reach of all those who are most vitally concerned about our architectural heritage.

Agnes Gilchrist should be thanked for her untiring efforts in putting the Society's architectural files in good order so that the committees concerned could perform their work more efficiently.

For every building listed in the Index, a "verification form" was filled out by an independent research worker and compared with the information previously listed. This work was initiated by Henry Hope Reed, Jr., who obtained the assistance of Mrs. Stewart Freeman as coordinator. She laid the groundwork, making it possible for John B. Schwartzman to take over her duties when she found she could no longer continue her good work.

Mr. Schwartzman should be credited with not only coordinating the work on "verifications" which had been expertly done by Christopher Jeffrey, Maud Dilliard, and Clay Lancaster, but with setting up the index of buildings in final form, indexing it, and also with assisting the editor in ascertaining certain facts for the bibliography. This was a formidable task, and he deserves all credit for seeing it through to a successful conclusion. Loring McMillen was kind enough to furnish us with information for our verifications relative to Staten Island.

In assembling the photographs, it was often found necessary to commission photographers to take certain buildings. Francis W. Roudebush has assisted the Committee on Historic Architecture from its first formation in the evaluation of photographs. John B. Bayley came to our rescue in filling the gaps where photos were either not suitable or not available. The photos which he took were invariably outstanding, as were the excellent detail shots taken by Charlotte La Rue. Wayne Andrews permitted us to draw on his invaluable collection, and credit is due to Constance Jacobs, who has taken photographs for the Society for many years. Margot Gayle and Christopher Jeffrey also took several excellent photographs for us. John Feulner, of the Underhill Studio, not only took photographs but assisted in making special enlargements and prints.

The carefully drawn maps which accompany the photographs were the work of Susanne Tauber and Ben Newman; they do much toward forming a fine, permanent record of building locations.

The editor was assisted in the preparation of his bibliography with suggestions as to format and additions by James G. Van Derpool, of the Landmarks Preservation Commission, and by Adolf K. Placzek, of the Avery Architectural Library at Columbia University. Thanks are due to the following persons and institutions for bibliographical information furnished to us: Gilbert A. Cam and Gunther Pohl of the New York Public Library, Daniel Chase of the Park Association of New York City, Robert Weinman and M. J. Amabile of the National Sculpture Society, James J. Heslin of the New-York Historical Society, Loring Mc-Millen of the Staten Island Historical Society, and Helen P. Bolman of the Long Island Historical Society.

Wolcott Andrews, landscape architect and Society board member, suggested that we should include photographs for the section dealing with parks. It was he who arranged for a helicopter to take the present-day photograph of the Esplanade and Mall in Central Park which we have shown in conjunction with the print from Valentine's Manual; and he who furnished the interesting information concerning the early use of the term "landscape architect."

For their thoughtful reading of the text, the editor wishes to thank Russell Lynes, Wayne Andrews, Knight Sturges, and Arnold L. Markowitz. Their suggestions contributed in no small measure toward the clarification of ideas and to making a difficult subject more readily understandable. Edward R. Finch Jr., Byron Golden, and Charles Magruder gave us valuable advice and the benefit of their knowledge.

To my wife, Frances, I am greatly indebted.

The text of this book, written by the editor, represents insofar as possible the ideals and objectives of the Municipal Art Society. It should not, however, be construed as necessarily embodying them throughout.

The Committee on Historic Architecture welcomes additions to the Index of Architecturally Notable Structures. Plans, data, and photographs of buildings suggested for inclusion should be sent to the Municipal Art Society of New York, marked for the attention of the Committee.

A. B.

New York, N.Y.
April, 1963

I. THE PAST

ODAY, as we wander the streets of New York, we come upon the architecture of the past, isolated examples that hold our attention. Some are masterpieces; others, interesting manifestations of their times, tell better than words how people lived, worked, and worshiped at various periods in this great city. We would like to think that not all these landmarks will be annihilated before that advancing wave of steel and glass which today is engulfing everything in its path. If everything is swept away and the continuity of our architectural heritage is obliterated, we shall have achieved only a catharsis and shall find ourselves confronted with an antiseptic monotony. Unfortunately, we have both the money and the power to level everything, destroying once cherished landmarks.

Our notable architecture represents an invaluable part of our cultural heritage, as important to future generations as the paintings and sculptures which we preserve in our museums and parks. Here, in *New York Landmarks*, we have attempted to make a survey of architecturally notable buildings worthy of preservation, with the hope that a plan may be devised whereby the finest of our heritage can still be preserved and integrated into the world of today. Thus our children might inherit at least fragments of our past in bricks and mortar, if only to give them historical perspective and a sense of awareness, so vital to all cultural achievement, that ours of today is not the only age of importance that ever existed.

The beauties of New York, unlike those of Paris, have always consisted of isolated buildings: freestanding masterpieces, hidden bits of the picturesque, often surrounded by mediocrity and lost in a sea of monotony.

When we finally began to come of age in the 'nineties, to build porticos, towers, and fountains, and to create meaningful vistas, they were built with forms borrowed from Europe. Much of this work was ingeniously adapted to American requirements, and it brought a certain lightness and gaiety to a city of "brownstones," laid out in never ending rows, on the monotonous grid plan which had been established by the City Commissioners in 1811.

Today, we are still ensnared in this grid plan with a new kind of monotony — that of steel and glass, sweeping in unrelieved rows up the avenues and into the side streets. It threatens to leave us in a scaleless vacuum in which man will become an ant, burrowing in and out of skyscrapers which no longer scrape the sky visually, being of nearly uniform height. Beautiful in themselves, certain buildings which glisten with a glassy elegance, such as Lever House, cease to be elegant when unrelieved by the masonry buildings which once surrounded them.

When all our buildings become glass cubes, drama will be lost to unending dreariness. The picturesque skyline of the latter part of the nineteenth century and the early twentieth is vanishing. In fact, the picturesque is today considered anathema, to such an extent that we seem to be bent on stamping out what little remains.

The towers and porticos arrived on the scene with the advent of the old Madison Square Garden, a piece of architecture seemingly borrowed from the treasure trove of Europe; yet it was a typically American solution, garbed in the ornament of another land. It contained two theatres, a restaurant, the main amphitheatre, and other facilities. The plan was virtually without precedent.

Our architects proceeded to bedeck their new world metropolis with handsome buildings set against the drab background of brick and chocolate brown. Rarely did they innovate in the realm of architectural detail, although Stanford White's base for the Farragut Monument in Madison Square and Louis Sullivan's detail for the cornice of the Bayard Building on Bleecker Street contributed a definitely new type of ornament.

What happened in New York was typical of what was happening all over the United States. We were growing too fast to await the full flowering of our vernacular art forms, so greatly admired by John Kouwenhoven. We could not await or understand the development of a native architecture such as that being evolved by Sullivan and Wright. Like the *nouveaux riches* of all ages, we sought a ready-made culture; unsure of our own taste and abashed by the learned pronouncements of "men of taste," we bought culture.

Russell Sturgis, the architect-historian, once said that if we could only have fifty years of plain, undecorated building, a new style might evolve itself naturally. Perhaps we are entering that period today, and perhaps the experiment will bear fruit — if man, like mouse, does not become lost in a scaleless vacuum.

John Mead Howells wrote a book entitled *Lost Examples of Colonial Architecture*. If we were to write such a book today about New York architecture, it would reveal countless masterpieces swept away by successive generations — by those tides of progress and destruction which began at the Battery and have, with constant onward flow, moved relentlessly north since Colonial times, sweeping away much of the best. Land values, unfortunately, have been the sole criterion of progress.

When we consider that Wall Street was once the outermost defensive bastion of a small town, we reconstruct the pattern of flow with ever increasing amazement, noting how commerce and fashion pushed ever northward, leaving Canal, Bleecker, and Fourteenth streets in their wake. Gone are the great shopping streets — the Ladies' Mile on Broadway, Twenty-third Street, and the emporiums of Sixth Avenue where ladies met at the fountain of Siegel-Cooper's palatial establishment. The push northward continues today, and the residential stronghold of upper Fifth Avenue, once believed impregnable, now yields to undistinguished apartment houses, where the altitude of the rent is considered more important than that of the living room ceiling. It is an exciting drama in which brick gave way to brownstone, brownstone to limestone, and everything today to the glistening, gossamer web of the all-glass curtain wall.

Nostalgia is the share of the old New Yorker when he walks through the streets and sees in fond memory some vanished church or residence as he stares blankly into the large plate-glass window of today's skyscraper. Where the entire complex of a city block, divided into twenty-five-foot lots, may now be occupied by one building, we realize what a little world of family residences and churches has been swept into oblivion. Some of these houses and some of these churches were architecturally noteworthy; and yet a certain house of the eighteen-seventies may be more completely lost to us today than certain Colonial houses, which were often quite similar to each other. It was this constant rebuilding which prompted Edith Wharton to remark that New York would become "as much a vanished city as Atlantis or the lowest layer of Schliemann's Troy."[*]

A way of life and a social structure crumbled, giving way to the feverish pace of today in which we are all caught, each in his own little circle. We lack time to stop, to appraise, to look about us, and to ask where we are going. To a few, the key to this question lies in a thorough knowledge of the past. The economist plots a chart to be able to base his predictions on known facts and figures derived from records carefully kept. The architectural historian keeps his records too; but the general public, though interested, does not usually have access to them and consequently views buildings as isolated entities set down by caprice. In reality, every style of architecture is an outgrowth of the economic and social background of its times. It is the surviving testimonial to a way of life, a period of growth and a period of transition, for all periods are in a constant state of flux.

Architectural history might be said to have begun with the Egyptians and to have ended ten minutes ago. We are writing it today. Every time we discover a new method of construction or a new material to create a new building which expresses our technology and our living requirements, we are writing that history and setting down a record for future archaeologists to read.

Henry Churchill, the town planner, once said of our cities that "the forces for change are relentless, the human aspirations remain the same. New forces are at work, which are incomprehensible except in terms of the past, if only for contrast, and are perhaps unpredictable on any score. The inability to predict should not make us fear understanding, rather it should make us seek it, for if we are to replan our cities we must know what it is that changes and why."[†]

[*]Edith Wharton, *A Backward Glance* (New York, D. Appleton-Century Co., Inc., 1934), p. 54.

[†] Henry S. Churchill, *The City Is the People* (New York, Harcourt, Brace & Company, Inc., 1945), p. 1.

Today there is a great awakening of interest in history and things historical. The American public is becoming proud of its heritage. Whether it is the fact that a period of prosperity is giving us more leisure to pursue cultural interests, or whether we are simply coming of age as a nation, is hard to say. Whatever the cause may be, the fact is that historical sites, old buildings, forts, covered bridges, and other visible manifestations of our past way of life are enjoying an unprecedented degree of attention from the public at large.

James Parton, the publisher, says that "hardly a decade ago history was almost universally regarded as 'dry as dust,' professional historians were men without much honor save in the Halls of Academe. Historical Societies were standard Hollywood symbols for any group of old fuddy-duds, and the flow of visitors through many of the nation's most beautifully preserved old houses would not have worn a hole in the entrance hall rug for another hundred years."* He cites the amazing figures of attendance at national shrines and historic houses, which have increased tremendously within the last eight or ten years.

The past is emerging as an active force for the present, and through our pride in our heritage and the breadth of understanding it should give us, we will emerge a wiser and happier nation. We will be secure in our knowledge of past triumphs and be better prepared to create new ones which will become our contribution to future generations.

* James Parton, "History as a Refuge from Today." *Maryland Historical Society Magazine,* Vol. 53, No. 1, March 1958.

II. AESTHETICS

IT HAS recently been considered important, in view of the undirected trends of contemporary architecture, to stop in our tracks and reappraise our achievement so we can more surely chart our course. We would like, if possible, to see where we are going and, more particularly, where we ought to go.

With this objective in view, the New York Chapter of the American Institute of Architects appointed a Design Committee to plan a "Conference on Aesthetic Responsibility."* The panel members were chosen from the arts, and the architects named, as their critics, men outside their field.

The results were extremely interesting; they have an objective, timeless quality which makes them equally applicable whether considered in retrospect or looking toward the future. Reference was made to "those retrovisionaries, the architectural historians," not in an uncomplimentary sense, but as a recognition of the fact that we must be capable of looking backward as well as forward to best appraise the future. This was a civilized approach to the problem we face in keeping a true sense of perspective.

We want to know why certain buildings are still aesthetically pleasing to us today, and we also ask whether they fulfilled their intended functions well when built. In this conference it was pointed out that what seems ugly today may very well be considered beautiful tomorrow. This applies not only to some of today's mammoth buildings of steel and glass but also to certain old buildings which we are all too ready to tear down, only to discover that our children consider them lost treasures.

Comparing architecture to other arts, it was said that, relative to painting, sculpture, poetry, and music, architecture is far less permanent: that, whereas works of art are preserved in museums and libraries in almost pristine condition, where many attain the status of masterpieces, only a few buildings, in conspicuous locations, attain this status; the majority, covered with soot and grime, are swept away by the demands of progress.

* "First Conference on Aesthetic Responsibility," *A.I.A. Journal*, Vol. 47, No. 6, June 1962, pp. 33–66. See esp. Russell Lynes, pp. 59–60.

The role of the architect, as the arbiter of taste whose professional duties are too complex to be readily understood by the public, came in for a fair share of responsibility for the aesthetics of our surroundings. The so-called "decision-makers" — the private owners, bankers, real estate men, and promoters who finance buildings and whose decisions often control the ultimate aesthetic success or the failure of a building — were also given their share of criticism. They were partly exonerated in that, it was said, they did not realize the full extent of their power. They honestly believed that they left artistic matters in the hands of the artists.

The fact that the artistic qualities of architecture must represent an integral part of an over-all solution, visualized in advance by the architect, has been true in all ages and remains so today.

This conference was a long-overdue opportunity for reappraisal, and it succeeded in pointing out the fact that, although a city of isolated masterpieces has its charms, architecture should be organized to reach out effectively and join hands with town planning. This is a primary requirement for achieving an aesthetically pleasing, coherent city.

In New York, architecture often did become unified in character, and this unity was, interestingly, achieved through the economics of mass production, with endless — and monotonous — rows of identical "brownstones." Yet similar rows of cast-iron business buildings produced the breath-taking endless vista of the mercantile district. The former was quite inappropriate, in that we expect a certain charm and variety in our residential areas, whereas we willingly accept a cold uniformity in the world of business.

Several attempts have been made to achieve coherent city blocks in New York without merely establishing monotonous repetition. These were schemes wherein several town houses were combined into one unified structure. We find examples of such designs in Colonnade Row on Lafayette Street, in the Villard Mansion on Madison Avenue, and in several city blocks of houses built in Harlem by McKim, Mead & White in the late nineteenth century, not to mention countless others now razed.

As we walk through the streets today, we should sharpen our architectural or aesthetic sensibilities by making note of many buildings; by criticizing the ugly ones and asking ourselves why they are ugly, by enjoying the beautiful, by learning lessons of form, texture, and color from past masterpieces, not to be copied but to serve as an inspiration.

Great architecture is not produced without true inspiration, and yet many different interpretations of it have been set forth. This age has arrogantly assumed that nothing can be learned from the past. To stand here, at a tiny point in time, looking only forward, seeking to create a new world by "inspiration" alone, is the height of folly. True inspiration cannot be created in a vacuum; it represents the sum total of everything we have ever seen or heard, upon which we then place our own interpretative stamp.

III. PRESERVATION
OF ARCHITECTURE

TODAY we hear much about the preservation of buildings. Communities both large and small are alarmed at the possibility that they may lose the last examples of their architecturally distinguished early buildings, and also that every last trace of intermediate periods of development may be lost. This refers to that mélange of styles which once graced "Main Street": buildings which are not necessarily great architecture according to our lights today, but which are representative of a succession of vanished eras and, as tastes do change, may be prized by our children or grandchildren.

To preserve any one of these buildings, a permanent tenant must be found. Merely to raise the money to save a building is not enough, as the cost of maintaining it, after a few years, might well equal the entire sum required to save it. Any group or society which raises a public subscription to save a building should attempt to keep its obligation down to the initial purchase price, or it may find that it loses both this and the entire building as well at the end of a few years, much to the disgust of the original contributors.

The Jefferson Market Courthouse, in New York, is a case in point. Had the committee which fought to save it not found a tenant, they could not have saved it at all. In this case, it was not even necessary to purchase the city-owned building but merely to find a city agency which could use it. It has now been established that it will become a branch library. In the case of a mansion of outstanding architectural distinction in a small town, it has often happened that a general public subscription is made to buy and save it and that a local historical society is only too glad to take it over as a permanent home.

Sometimes the economic forces are too great, as in the case of great railroad terminals, hotels, and office buildings. In such cases it is often possible, as it was with Grand Central Station, to save at least a portion of the original structure, incorporating it into a new scheme.

"Main Street" is the area most likely to be rebuilt beyond recognition in prosperous towns where each merchant, quite logically, wishes to remodel his own building to present an up-to-date appearance. This does not prevent us from saving notable architecture on the back streets before all examples of all eras have either disintegrated beyond repair or been completely "modernized."

The planning board of every community should have an architectural advisor who can designate buildings worthy of protection, so that where possible these buildings may be saved. Any preservation plan should also include statuary, fountains in parks, and outstanding groups of buildings built as a unified whole, which form an attractive part of the cityscape.

New York is most fortunate in that a commission has recently been established by the Mayor to designate notable examples of architecture throughout the entire city. It is known as the Landmarks Preservation Commission and is headed by a distinguished architect, assisted by a well-known architectural historian. Their recommendations will help to establish new criteria for the evaluation of architectural landmarks and will eventually designate many buildings in all five boroughs which are not even included here, documenting and photographing them for future reference.

Today the bulldozer in a few hours can wreck the masterpiece of an era, perhaps the sole surviving example; and, if no controls are established, it might level every last vestige of our architectural heritage.

Except for the pioneer efforts of the American Scenic and Historic Preservation Society, this attempt to establish building categories in *New York Landmarks*, and the Mayor's newly appointed commission, preservation in New York City has always been a hit-or-miss affair. This is probably because New York is so big, and the economic forces so great, that the residents have always felt that it was quite beyond them to save anything except by tackling individual, isolated problems as they arose.

In other cities greater strides have recently been made — particularly in Philadelphia, where history is happily married to architectural distinction. There, the Independence Mall scheme has blossomed and spread to include blocks of surrounding buildings. More important is the fact that a comprehensive plan has been made, and that town planners have worked with historians in establishing it. The National Park Service has lent its weight and considerable resources to the realization of a part of this project.

Providence, Rhode Island, has come forth with its study *College Hill*, produced jointly by the City Plan Commission, the Providence Preservation Society, and the federal Housing and Home Finance Agency. This is undoubtedly one of the finest studies produced to date, a worthy prototype for other communities. It is particularly noteworthy from our point of view, as it analyzes and illustrates in considerable detail the existing architectural landmarks, while at the same time setting forth its new plans for urban redevelopment. In this study, new planning is carefully integrated with a program for the preservation of noteworthy structures and districts.

Beacon Hill, in Boston, had already been the subject of a careful study when that city found itself confronted with the reality of a comprehensive redevelopment plan. A committee has now been named to study and make recommendations relative to the preservation of notable architecture and groups of buildings worthy of preservation. It remains to be seen whether redevelopment and preservation activities are coordinated there.

In anticipation of proposed redevelopment, Brooklyn Heights began a survey several years ago to document buildings adjudged worthy of preservation. This survey led to the publication of *Old Brooklyn Heights,* by Clay Lancaster, a book which covers most of the pre-Civil War architecture of that section in great detail.

One of the first city studies which attempted to place buildings in categories, as we do here in *New York Landmarks,* was *This Is Charleston,* a small book of considerable significance which appeared in 1944. It contained a photograph of each building of note and a history of the city. Our categories tend, generally, to follow those which it established, as follows: buildings of national importance, those of value to the city, and those simply designated as valuable. It went on to point out notable buildings and, finally, buildings worthy of mention. This book was the result of a survey undertaken by the Charleston Civic Services Committee, with historical text by Samuel Gaillard Stoney. It was published by the Carolina Art Association.

Many other cities have made commendable efforts to record noteworthy architecture, whether by such formalized studies as those outlined above or through the publication of monographs on individual buildings written by architects or architectural historians. These books have often been published by means of private, local subscriptions which were raised when no commercial publisher could be found.

Federal recognition of architecture has usually come indirectly through existing organizations or through commissions set up for specific purposes. The activities of the American Institute of Architects, in Washington, D.C., have kept the federal government informed as to pressing problems of the profession and have been of inestimable value in this regard. For years they have espoused the cause of preservation, but it was not until the establishment of the Historic American Buildings Survey, during the depression, that any direct federal recognition was obtained on a nationwide scale. This agency was set up under the National Park Service of the Department of the Interior, and it produced a priceless record of buildings, many of which have been razed since they were recorded. Although we may be coming of age as a nation, we have never established those broad controls which operate to protect public monuments in many of the countries of Europe.

With the accession of Louis-Philippe to the throne of France, in 1830, his minister of the interior, Guizot, established the now famous *Commission des Monuments Historiques,* which by designating monuments brought under its control many of the most notable structures of France.*

As a court of common appeals, we have the National Trust for Historic Preservation, chartered by act of Congress in 1949. Supported by tax-exempt contributions and membership dues, its budget does not permit of the maintenance of more than a few carefully selected historic buildings, such as "Woodlawn Plantation" in Virginia and some others. It lacks the power to stay the hand of the wrecker, but it does perform the very important

---

* Bibliothèque Nationale, *Prosper Mérimée.* Paris, 1953. See esp. Chap. III, pp. 40ff., "L'Inspecteur Général des Monuments Historiques."

function of acting as a clearing house of information, giving advice from its broad experience and, through its magazine and newsletter, signalizing pending demolitions of notable structures throughout the nation.

On the local scene, the following organizations officially or unofficially contribute to the cause of preservation: The American Scenic and Historic Preservation Society, the Municipal Art Society, the Fine Arts Federation, the Art Commission, the National Sculpture Society, the National Shrines Advisory Board, the New York Chapter of the American Institute of Architects, the New York Society of Architects, the Architectural League, the Planning Commission, the Fifth Avenue Association, the New York Community Trust, the New York Park Association, and the Landmarks Preservation Commission. Museums and historical societies throughout Greater New York are always particularly sympathetic to the cause of preserving that which is most noteworthy in the city.

In addition to buildings which have been razed, it is also interesting to consider the case of those which have been defaced or hidden by modernizations. These metamorphoses range from those cases where the entire outer skin is removed and replaced by curtain wall or other modernizations, to those which are simply enveloped, intact, in a new coat of glistening porcelain enamel or some other twentieth-century veneer. Perhaps the most tragic cases are those in which the columns are simply chopped off at street level to provide wider show windows. Such was the case of Tiffany's former store at Thirty-seventh Street and Fifth Avenue. Those which are deprived of their outer skins are to all intents and purposes dead and past recall, while those which are only veneered may well prove the joy of future archaeologists.

It is interesting to note, with regard to buildings which are threatened with demolition to make way for some new skyscraper, that some of the largest and most imposing structures are often doomed, despite the fact that they may be surrounded by blocks of third-rate three- and four-story buildings. How much better the city would eventually look if the rabble of low, undistinguished buildings could give way to the new skyscraper, while preserving the larger, respectable one. A good example of this phenomenon is the threatened demolition of the Hudson Terminal Buildings on lower Church Street. Here we can only assume that, the lots being already assembled, it is considered worth while to tear down such substantial structures while the low-lying blocks remain. Even though the large buildings, in this case, are of only moderate interest architecturally, they represent respectability and a colossal investment. This is typical of the uncontrolled destruction and waste which goes on every day of the week in this great city.

Preservation is our responsibility and must be kept within the bounds of reason. It should be based on standards of evaluation determined by those best qualified to designate what should be preserved.

IV. PARKS, SQUARES, AND VISTAS

THE proudest possession of which our city can boast is its system of parks, those dots and belts of greenery which make life in summer tolerable and which give us space and a vantage point from which to view what we have wrought. Hemmed in by our narrow streets, we rarely see or have an opportunity to appreciate the best of our architecture.

The park is our place for relaxation, for enjoyment, and for the pursuit of health; if it did not fulfill any of these requirements, there would not be any particular reason for its existence. For a park to best serve its purpose, its usefulness must be balanced against the time element — that is, the time involved in getting there from one's place of residence within the city. Centrally located or urban parks are generally closest to hand and most easily reached. To reach perimeter or fringe parks may take considerable time. A visit to an outlying or picnic park may require making a definite plan in advance and setting out on an expedition.

A park which is located only a few blocks away from one's place of residence is a readily reachable asset; but, when the nearest park is more than four blocks away, its use is generally postponed until more time is available. To be of maximum use to the city dweller, a park must have day-to-day availability, although more distant parks perform a valuable secondary function.

Thomas Holmes's plan, laid out for William Penn's new city of Philadelphia in 1682, achieved the maximum in usefulness. It made its small, block-size parks readily available to all its inhabitants simultaneously, as the spacing of the squares was such that they were approximately equidistant and relatively close together. Savannah, Georgia, as planned in the early eighteenth century by General Oglethorpe, provided a somewhat similar scheme, with its parks even more closely spaced.

The so-called "Commissioners' Plan" for New York City, laid out in 1811, established a rectilinear grid plan for approximately all of that portion of Manhattan lying above

Washington Square. The avenues, widely spaced, ran north-south. They were intended to relieve the traffic from the closely spaced east-west streets which served the river traffic, at that time a primary factor in the life of the city. A few small parks were set out in a most haphazard manner throughout the city, while the present site of Central Park was to have been occupied by a solid mass of city blocks. The only concession to open air was a space indicated as "The Parade," extending from Third to Seventh Avenue and from Twenty-third to Thirty-fourth Street — now reduced to Madison Square as we know it today. The origin of most of our parks was usually utilitarian. They were either military parade grounds or cemeteries laid out for the poor, the potter's fields of a former generation. The Bloomingdale Road, later to be renamed Broadway, was the one street of any note which defied the new grid plan. As it was a vital artery, it was allowed to remain, cutting through the grid on a slant. This long, diagonal avenue created a series of tiny triangular parks, too small to be of much use; small islands disrupting the regularity of the pattern.

It is only in our parks that we can really see and enjoy our city architecture. We can stand off at a distance and see buildings as buildings, not merely as a row of ever disappearing façades. New York, unlike Paris, has few charming vistas. A vista, to be enjoyed, should eventually be terminated by some object, a statue or a building, which will lend scale and interest to the otherwise interminable length of repetitive monotony. Here again, we find that our closed vistas either were the result of happy accident, or were due to the fact that an oversized building was set down covering two blocks and interrupting what had once been a street.

The parks themselves, as oases of greenery, have often provided the setting for statues, flagpoles, fountains, and other such nonutilitarian delights of man, objects which he can enjoy during his short moments of peace and relaxation.

Practically every park in the city has, at one time or another, become a target for projects, ranging from cheap concessions to the most elaborately planned structures. We can only marvel today that they have all remained relatively free of such encumbrances. Central Park, due to its vast size, has accumulated over the years a weird assortment of structures. Many of these no longer exist, while the more appropriate ones, such as the Museum of Art and the zoo, do not seem too much out of place. The threat of invasion is real and is a constant danger to our small inheritance of greenery.

Among the urban parks which are located in residential districts, there are few which were not at one time part of the open countryside. Our first park, Bowling Green, which lay just outside the original fort, was established in 1734 when the Common Council rented this small area to three gentlemen for the purpose of establishing a bowling green for the entertainment of the local burghers.

City Hall Park was at this time known as "The Commons," a public pasturage or grazing ground for cattle outside the limits of the small city. Most of the uptown urban parks were originally laid out as real estate ventures, with the desirable adjoining lots laid out around them. Several had the added inducement of being built as enclosures to which those property owners facing them held the keys. Gramercy Park is today the sole survivor of this type of park. Some of the parks, such as Stuyvesant and Washington squares, were cut in two by north-south avenues; whereas Gramercy and Mount Morris parks defied the avenues which would have bisected them, forcing the streets to go around. Recently, Washington Square residents have fought and won a valiant battle to have all traffic banned from the center of the square.

Union Square and Madison Square are quite similar, having in common the fact that both are bounded on the west by Broadway, with all its attendant odd shapes and leftover triangles. They are both formal, urban squares which, although no longer residential in character, are nonetheless still large enough to permit us to enjoy the buildings which surround them. Their spacing, combined with that of Gramercy Park, would have made an ideal pattern if it had been adhered to for the length and breadth of the city.

We may be shocked to realize that, despite our dearth of urban parks, we have lost four of note since the original Commissioners' Plan was laid out: Hamilton, Manhattan, and Franklin squares and Saint John's Park, later renamed Hudson Square. In terms of land area, this was a very small loss, as we have since gained the vast acreage of Central Park. But to those who value greenery in residential or commercial neighborhoods, the loss of these urban parks is not really compensated for by our Central Park, nor, except to youth, by the blacktopped playgrounds which have happily been added throughout the city in such considerable numbers.

The urban park or square is a formal park and so is the popular promenade. The promenade is, historically speaking, represented by the Battery, the old "lungs of the city." It was the resort of all and sundry for taking the air of a hot summer's night, for the early morning saunter along the sea wall, and for the noontide stroll under its central shade trees. All of this we had when the city was small, before Central Park had even been thought of. Much as Trinity and Saint Paul's churchyards delight the noontide stroller today, in the heart of the business district, so did Green-Wood Cemetery, Brooklyn, delight the youth of the 1850's, where, among its lakes, small hills, cliffs, crags, and monuments, many a tender courtship flourished.

Today our promenades are blacktopped and surrounded by handball courts and jungle gyms, but, despite their hard aspect, they fulfill a very real function, and in time this aspect will be softened by the growth of their sapling trees. Two of the best of these promenade-parks are that on the lower East River, extending from Fourteenth Street to Jackson Street, and that on the upper West Side, between 72nd Street and 125th Street, running parallel to and below Riverside Drive.

The picnic park is the park one plans ahead of time to visit when one has hours to spare. Because of their very considerable sizes and great widths, Central Park, Manhattan, Prospect Park, Brooklyn, and Van Cortlandt Park, Bronx, fall largely into this category, although the Fifth Avenue and Central Park West sides of Central Park are two of our finest promenades.

Of all our Manhattan parks, Central Park is undoubtedly the most interesting, as it was consciously planned as a park and as it introduced many novel features when it was first laid out. After considering a site on the East River at Jones' Wood, the Legislature finally passed a bill in 1853, authorizing the creation of a park to be located between Fifth and Eighth avenues and 63rd and 100th streets. Later, the park was officially extended to 59th and 110th streets. The site of the park was described as a sort of no-man's land containing some five thousand squatters' shanties before it was developed.

A commission was formed in 1857, including among its members Andrew Haswell Green, the father of Greater New York, who later served as its president. The commission held a competition for a comprehensive plan for the development of the park. This competition was won by Plan no. 33, entitled "Greensward," designed by Frederick Law Olmsted and Calvert Vaux. It included many novel features, such as the four east-west transverse roads which were dropped below the level of the park to avoid interference with pedestrians and those who might be riding horseback or driving in carriages on the inner drives which made the circuit of the park. This far-sighted planning was doubly significant as it was initiated long before the motor age, at a time when city traffic consisted only of carriages.

The whole scheme, with one exception, was romantic in concept, with free-flowing paths, walks, and drives carried through and around "natural" features such as hills, ponds, cliffs, and groves of trees and arbors, many of which had been artificially created to give the feeling that one was passing through a wild, natural setting. All the bridges were of different design to further enhance the apparent naturalism of the setting. Extensive lawns swept out over a gently undulating landscape in which the Croton reservoirs formed the largest single features.

Within this asymmetrical scheme was set out a single piece of formal, symmetrical landscape gardening. This consisted of the Esplanade and the Mall. The former, located opposite Seventy-second Street, began at the level of the lake and provided a setting for the centrally placed Bethesda Fountain by Emma Stebbins, behind which rose a double flight of stairs leading up to the Mall — a grand double alley of trees, much in the French tradition. Jacob Wrey Mould assisted Calvert Vaux in designing the architectural features of the Esplanade, using detail which to American eyes must have seemed highly original, although it had its prototype in Victorian England. The whole concept was very grand and was marred only by the fact that the design permitted traffic to cross the park at grade at Seventy-second Street, without employing the usual underpasses, thus creating a pedestrian hazard at the top of the steps where one entered the Mall. It may be presumed that where only slow-moving carriages were concerned this was justifiable, as the planners doubtless wished those arriving by carriage to have the most dramatic possible approach to the Esplanade, by descending the grand staircases. The Esplanade was designed to serve as an outdoor music hall, a setting for fireworks or any such program of festivities as might be desired.

Despite many controversies, the wall around the park remained low and the gates simple and unostentatious, as originally planned. Proposals have been made from time to time to rebuild various gates, each of which bore a name, to suit the latter-day fashions of the

Esplanade and Mall, Central Park: Photographed from a Helicopter, 1962

Esplanade and Mall, Central Park: An Artist's Rendering from *Valentine's Manual*, 1864

times, but they were always defeated by those who appreciated the rustic quality of the original scheme.

The distances in Central Park are considerable and the whole concept outstanding for its day. Its great genius lay in the fact that it brought into the heart of the city the wild rambles, the hills and ponds of the back country, giving the city dweller a taste of remote rural pleasures.

In 1857, when Olmsted won the competition with the architect Vaux, he was only thirty-five years old and had been known primarily as a writer, economist, and philanthropist, and lastly as a landscape gardener. It was highly significant that, in 1862, the New York City Central Park Commission used the term "landscape architect" in referring to Olmsted and to Vaux, a title which Olmsted retained in his later works. This was probably the first notable instance in which the usual title "landscape gardener" was replaced by "landscape architect" in this country.*

Perimeter parks are generally of elongated shape, following the outer profile of the city. In Manhattan, they are usually located at the waterfront or along some feature of topographical variance, such as a cliff or high bluff which tends, in itself, to separate two parts of the city. They include both East and West Side developments as well as Inwood Hill Park and Morningside, Saint Nicholas, and High Bridge parks.

Overflow parks might be said to be those to which the city population makes excursion for a day's outing. These include Randall's and Ward's islands for sports, Liberty Island for sightseeing, and Van Cortlandt Park for those who seek a rural setting without wishing to make a foray into the ever receding countryside.

Fort Tryon Park, which lies above 193rd Street, has a high plateau with a superb view of the Hudson and the Palisades. At its northern end lies the Cloisters, a section of the park which might be described as a cultural experiment, combining some of the art treasures of the Old World with an almost perfect natural setting, readily accessible to the urban population. The Cloisters is now a branch of the Metropolitan Museum and was presented to the city by John D. Rockefeller, Jr.

Fort Tryon Park was originally notable as the site of the fort and later, of the small castle built by a certain A. C. Richards in 1864, known as "Wood Cliff." It was renamed Libbey Castle for a subsequent owner and finally was absorbed by the estate of the millionaire sportsman C. K. G. Billings. His palatial mansion burned in 1926, leaving only the spectacular arcaded entrance to his driveway off Riverside Drive as a reminder of that establishment.

A consideration of vantage points from which we can enjoy our architecture would include, in addition to the urban park, the vista. The endless vista is the view we obtain with the grid plan from so many of our streets and avenues, where the end of the street simply disappears over the horizon, with no terminal feature. In Paris the problem of creating attractive terminal features was carefully studied and included in the designs of Baron

* L. H. Bailey, *Standard Cyclopedia of Horticulture* (New York, Macmillan Company, 1937), p. 1784.

The Cloisters, Fort Tryon Park

Bethesda Fountain and Esplanade, Central Park

Haussmann. In New York our vistas were rarely studied or planned; however, we have a few charming views such as that of Grace Church tower closing the upper end of lower Broadway where it changes direction. Another instance of a closed vista occurs where a building covers two blocks, thus terminating a street. We immediately think of the New York Public Library, the south side of Grand Central Station, and the east front of Pennsylvania Station. The most obvious type of termination is the monument placed in the middle of the street, such as that at Columbus Circle, or the triumphal arches at Washington Square and at the Grand Army Plaza in Brooklyn. The Grand Central Office Building, at the lower end of Park Avenue, closes the vista completely in a visual sense, while the new Pan-Am Building provides the terminal feature when seen from a point far up the avenue, where it becomes effective long after we have lost sight of the smaller building. We are dealing with building heights and a scale so different from those of the European capitals that we must establish a whole new set of criteria.

We also have the off-center vista, usually caused by the slicing diagonal of Broadway. Here we have the tall building which sits just off to one side of the avenue but which forms, nonetheless, a conspicuous feature of it. This would include such buildings as the Times

Tower and the Flatiron Building, although there are other instances of it such as the Jefferson Market Courthouse with its picturesque clock tower, a landmark at West Tenth Street and Sixth Avenue.

A new feature, which tends to lend further interest to the endless vista, is the setback building with a small plaza in front of it. The building is still included in the vista but it lends a new interest to the street, as is the case with the Seagram Building on Park Avenue. Two such buildings, located opposite each other, would create an area of light and sunshine which would be almost equal to that of a small square. Even where such little plazas are staggered, the view is enlivened by alternate sparkles of sunshine along an otherwise drab vista.

As we walk along a street or an avenue, we are led on ever further by such points of interest. Our curiosity is aroused by the setback, we want to get to that sunlit object seen dimly at the end, whatever it may prove to be.

Over the years our city will grow in interest as planners abandon the hard, rectilinear profiles of the old grid plan while retaining its advantages. Lever House set the pace and proved that a notable landmark, though perhaps costly, is also an advertisement. Certain new buildings are adopting free forms which introduce breath-taking possibilities; and, although none of this is part of a grand master plan, it is part of our normal development and, as such, an expression of our life and times.

V. SCULPTURE

SCULPTURE in New York has run a wide gamut of expression. It began with those eighteenth-century manifestations, the equestrian statue of George III in Bowling Green which was pulled down by the revolutionary mob, and the toga-clad figure of William Pitt, Earl of Chatham, which was decapitated by British soldiers outraged at the wrecking of the statue of George III.

Most early sculpture consisted of free-standing figures, with or without pedestals, for which Central Park later became the principal repository. The cemeteries provided their share of bas-reliefs, urns, and busts, but it was not until the eighteen-sixties that sculpture was to any extent combined with architecture, under the influence of the French Second Empire. We think of such buildings as the recently razed (Fisk's) Grand Opera House, at West Twenty-third Street and Eighth Avenue; the old National Park Bank, which once stood opposite Saint Paul's Church on Broadway; and the Civic Repertory Theater, formerly located at 105 West Fourteenth Street. Also typical of the late 'sixties were the awkward granite or metal war memorials to be seen, even today, on the greens of most New England towns.

It was with the return from Paris of the architects who had been trained at the Ecole des Beaux Arts that sculpture began to be widely used as a basic adjunct to architecture. Bas-reliefs in panels and arch spandrels, pediments replete with figures, and statues on balustrades of all sizes and descriptions now appeared, executed in varying degrees of competence. The ingenuity of our native sculptors was taxed to rival the glories of Europe, and in many instances work of outstanding beauty was achieved.

Attilio Piccirilli evoked a definite mood with his superb figures for the Maine Memorial at Columbus Circle, while A. A. Weinman enhanced the truly Roman grandeur of the great Chambers Street arch of the Municipal Building. Saint-Gaudens' equestrian statue of General Sherman, a free-standing masterpiece, lent new beauty to Fifth Avenue at Fifty-ninth Street. French's "Alma Mater" at Columbia University provided a staid type of elegance which was suitable as an introduction to the Low Library. In addition, Keck, Mac-

Monnies, and many others contributed to the classical grandeur that was New York before 1914. A more highly individualized style was to be found in the work of Chester Beach, Anna Huntington, G. G. Barnard, and Sherry Fry, while Paul Manship was soon to strike his own note of modernity.

In the first decades of the twentieth century, experiments were made in stylizations, many of which were exhibited in the Armory Show of 1913. Our sculptors attempted to simplify the expression of form, to introduce color, and to make experiments in texture and in the use of materials. To Paul Jennewein and to Leon V. Solon goes much of the credit for the serious study of color in sculpture. In the meantime, a host of ceramicists ran riot with figurines, tile bas-reliefs, and borders set in stucco walls in the early 'twenties. This work resulted in a sort of art-conscious Italianism which, in its superficiality, led nowhere but produced a sort of spurious charm in the "Beauty Rows" of the times.

Beginning in the 'thirties, sculptors proceeded to divorce their art from architecture. They were no longer willing to serve in a subordinate role but sought an individualistic expression. Each piece of sculpture was to have a setting of its own or was to be set, free, in a wall of brick or stone, provided by the architect but not controlled by panels, belt courses, arch spandrels, or other restraining elements of architecture.

The sculptors had emancipated themselves, and, as they considered ornament to be beneath their calling, they found themselves almost totally removed from the architect's world. Meanwhile the architects were beginning to divest their buildings of ornament, making the gap between themselves and the sculptors even greater than before. Yet by the mid-'forties there were signs of a new integration wherein stabiles and interior fountains, with all their adjuncts, were once again joined with architecture, even though their marriage was less basic and more in the nature of a practical accommodation.

VI. THE STYLES

WE MAY well ask what it is that entitles a building or a statue to be designated a "landmark." Actually there are two reasons. The first is historical. That George Washington slept in a house assures it a place in history, as does literary fame — the house lived in by Tom Paine, Edgar Allen Poe, or O. Henry.

The second reason, which concerns us here, is the architectural distinction of any structure. A house may be considered for its architecturally noteworthy features, regardless of the fame or obscurity of its occupants.

It is hard for the layman to consider the aesthetics of architecture as he would those of a painting or a piece of sculpture because the practical, functional requirements of architecture assert themselves at once. This is as it should be in making any intelligent appraisal of our architecture. We should be aware of the forces that shaped it, the aspirations of the times, and the so-called "styles" of architecture which are the outward manifestations of its creation.

Today there is an awakening interest in architecture. The sensitive observer wants to know what labels he should apply to the buildings he sees around him. He is aware of the differences between buildings, but he would like to know how to designate them — what periods of time they represent and what type of life produced them.

Architectural styles are regarded by many as superficial appliqués, as things borrowed or even stolen from past cultures, alien things which belong to other peoples and are un-American.

Whatever the origins of our styles, we must agree that, with the given set of conditions under which we lived, they did come into being and they do represent our architectural heritage. Much as we would like to have seen a national, indigenous style evolve, the fact remains that, with few exceptions, it did not do so until the twentieth century. We cannot rewrite history as we feel it should have developed; we must accept it as it was and try to understand it.

Actually, the time element has always been a factor in our architectural development. We were moving too fast, we had too much money to spend to permit a simple, vernacular architecture to evolve. We demanded the best; and our architects, unable or unwilling to originate new forms, borrowed the superficials from Europe, while making extremely ingenious adaptations to a new set of requirements. This process produced buildings which, if studied in plan, were often quite original and fairly well suited to our way of life.

Later, when we did originate new building forms, such as the skyscraper and the high apartment house, we found ourselves faced with such a completely new set of requirements that we evolved a new structural system, a new ornament, and a new style. It was probably the uniformity or American quality of this new style which prompted the French architect Le Corbusier to write, in 1936, that "New York has a style, has style, is mature enough to have acquired style. There are not just ragged things here; there is quality. A spirit is asserting itself; . . . the people, the shops, the products, the architecture, have achieved a character which is grand, intense and healthy."*

INTRODUCTORY

A brief analysis of the styles of architecture, which followed each other in such rapid succession, may help us to clarify our thinking about architecture relative to our knowledge of history.

The following discussion of architectural styles is intended to aid as an interpretation of the styles listed in the Index of Architecturally Notable Structures in Greater New York, to be found under Section VIII. It should enable anyone who is interested in going beyond this Index to arrive at some understanding of our early architecture, of the Revivals, and of what constituted Eclecticism. In many cases divisions and the periods of time assigned to the various styles will seem arbitrary; however, in order to arrive at anything approximating a clear picture of stylistic development, we must cleave to broad lines and refer to the exception only in passing. In order to illustrate best the work of certain styles, we have included references to some New York buildings which do not appear in our Index.

An elementary attempt has been made to lead the reader on to explore new fields and to broaden his architectural horizons.

COLONIAL ARCHITECTURE

As its name implies, Colonial architecture was the architecture of the colonies, imported from the mother country. In the United States, this term has been used very loosely. To most people today, it conjures up visions of a house with four white columns in front, brick walls, white trim, and shutters. Actually, such a house could only belong to the Georgian or later phase of our Colonial architecture.

* Le Corbusier, *When the Cathedrals Were White — A Journey to the Country of Timid People*. New York, Reynal & Hitchcock, 1947.

That architecture which was most truly "colonial" was the early Colonial; that of the mediaeval-type house, such as the House of Seven Gables in Salem, the French Colonial of New Orleans, the Spanish Colonial of Florida and California, and the Dutch Colonial of New York.

The Dutch Colonial, of which most of the remaining examples are to be found in Brooklyn, is typified in Manhattan by the Dyckman House. The most conspicuous feature of this style of architecture was the wide eave extending out over the front of the house, above which the main roof was generally swept forward in a gentle downward curve. It usually had a regular gable-ended roof, but some of these seemingly Dutch houses had gambrel roofs which have been traced to other origins.*

Many of these houses had side wings, aligned in the same axis as the main house, but often this small side wing was the oldest part of the house. The walls and roof were generally covered with wood shingles, while the chimneys were of brick with capacious fireplaces designed for cooking with cranes and spits. These Dutch Colonial houses, built in the seventeenth and eighteenth centuries, were usually farmhouses in open fields when built, although many are in the heart of the city today.

Of the yellow-brick step-gabled town houses, none remains today in Manhattan, but we have many old prints which show the solid wood shutters, the "Dutch doors," and the ornamental strap-iron reinforcements and "dates" which were such a conspicuous feature of their exterior walls. The roofs were often of tile, and some of the buildings, such as the Stadt Huys, the sugar houses, and the churches were quite sizable.

Early American architecture, as we often refer to it, represents those vernacular or native forms which were of the colonies but were not colonial imports. They were largely developed in this country and were modified to suit local climatic conditions. They are represented by the salt-box of New England, the stone farmhouse of Pennsylvania, and the brick or stone farmhouse of New York, including those simple brick and wood structures in both the South and New England. They were roughly contemporaneous with the Dutch Colonial and were the products of a colonial society, limited to materials at hand, primitive tools, and an indistinctly remembered ancestry.

Georgian

Georgian Colonial architecture, with its rich detail, was derived from the England of the Georges. In this country, it roughly paralleled the reigns of George I and George II (1714–1760), although it actually extended to about 1790, overlapping the first half of the reign of George III. In New York it is best exemplified by Saint Paul's Chapel, which was influenced by the work of James Gibbs in London; by the Morris-Jumel house at 160th Street on Washington Heights; and by the Van Cortlandt Manor in Van Cortlandt Park.

* Thomas T. Waterman reminds us that the gambrel roof was little known in Holland and that where we find one in this country, the house was probably not Dutch but French Huguenot in origin. Consequently, many houses we have always assumed to be Dutch were probably French. See p. 201 of Waterman's book, *The Dwellings of Colonial America*, Chapel Hill, University of North Carolina Press, 1950.

These are among the few remaining pre-Revolutionary Georgian buildings left to us today in New York. Fraunces Tavern has been restored to its presumed original appearance.

Georgian church architecture was the most elaborate. It often included, in the interior, freestanding Corinthian columns supporting block entablatures, designed to match the continuous entablatures supported by pilasters at the sidewalls. The large Palladian windows, broken pediments over doorways, and other English Renaissance features were also much in evidence. On the exterior, low, pitched roofs might be surrounded by low balustrades, while towers made the transition from square bases to octagonal superstructures with a variety of consoles, urns, and pediments to adorn them. The corners of the masonry walls were formed with dressed stone quoins. Where small stones were used in the walls, as in Saint Paul's Chapel, the quoins and dressed stone door and window frames did much to stabilize the building both structurally and visually.

The Georgian tradition in New York survived in two churches which, oddly enough, introduced pointed Gothic windows in their sidewalls. Saint Augustine's Chapel and the Church of the Sea and Land are the two examples of this Georgian-Gothic style. Although they were built during the later Federal period, they were Georgian in their main massing and form. The explanation of this introduction of Gothic forms may well stem from the existence of a book published in 1747 by Batty Langley, a British architect, which was entitled *Gothic Architecture Improved by Rules and Proportions*, or from one of the early nineteenth-century architectural handbooks.

FEDERAL

Federal architecture was the architecture of the new republic. It covered the period from slightly before the inauguration of George Washington as President, in 1789, to approximately 1825, coinciding in its last years with the elegant period of the regency in England (1811–1820).

In many respects it differed from the rich Georgian architecture of the colonies, too often associated with Tory rule and the Loyalists. It was our architectural declaration of independence, and, in its elegant new simplicity, it typified the best we could produce. Again it was derivative in its basic forms, but the detail was often highly original and, when furnished by a Duncan Phyfe, unique. Delicacy of detail and attenuation of form were among the salient characteristics of this new style influenced by the brothers Adam.

Pedimented doorways gave way to those with leaded side lights surmounted by half-circle or elliptical fan lights set in flush walls without notable projections. Corinthian columns generally yielded to Doric, and it must have seemed to the public eye that an elegant new austerity had swept the land.

The old Federal Hall, designed by Major l'Enfant, which once occupied the site of the Federal Hall National Memorial (U.S. Subtreasury Building), was a fine example of Federal architecture, and it was here, on the front balcony, that Washington took the oath of office. City Hall, although belonging to the Federal Period, shows considerable French

influence, contributed by Joseph Mangin, the French architect who collaborated with John McComb in its design.

The Commandant's House in the New York Navy Yard in Brooklyn, Hamilton Grange at 141st Street, Manhattan, and the Gracie Mansion on the East River are fine examples of wooden Federal country houses. The old James Watson house, which until recently has served as Our Lady of the Rosary at 7 State Street,* is one of the best preserved of our Federal town houses, although it was an unusual piece of design and not altogether typical. A large symmetrical brick house of the period may be seen at 45 Grove Street in Greenwich Village — complete with delicate marble window lintels, although the windows at the first floor were altered at a later date.

THE REVIVALS (GENERAL)

Revival styles of architecture in the United States must be differentiated from those which are "survivals." Survival architectures are those in which a native tradition was re-membered and re-created in the new colonies by craftsmen and architects who had actually built such buildings in their native lands or who had been trained by those who had. The architectural styles which we have discussed up to this point — except Early American and the Federal style — might be described as survival architectures.

The introduction of revival styles in this country represented a self-conscious re-creation of architectural styles of other countries. They were usually introduced here out of admiration, literary or political, for the countries which had originated them; or by architects and other travelers who had actually seen them. It was symptomatic of our awakening interest in foreign cultures and civilizations that we not only accepted but actively sought out new forms for our architecture.

It was characteristic of our revival styles that the first one to come to us was the Greek Revival. Here we sought to reproduce the forms of Greek architecture, quite regardless of its suitability, primarily as a symbol of our sympathy with the Greek struggle for independence. Next came a wave of romantic styles, including the Gothic Revival, seemingly a reaction against our classical past. This new romanticism inaugurated the freedom of the plan.

A turning point in our architectural development came with the World's Columbian Exposition at Chicago, in 1893, when a new era of classical and Renaissance architecture was inaugurated almost to the exclusion of other more romantic styles. This spelled the death knell of the Revival styles which, by 1893, were almost totally extinct except for such hardy survivors as the Romanesque Revival, making way for that which some choose to call the American Renaissance and for the Age of Eclecticism.

Greek Revival

The Greek Revival, which began about 1830, may be described as a second attempt to

* To become the shrine of Blessed Elizabeth Seton.

establish a national style, as we had done in 1789 with the Federal style. Seeking a new mode of expression, we followed with interest Lord Byron's participation in the Greek struggle for independence from the Turks.* Stuart and Revett had published *The Antiquities of Athens* in England between the years 1762 and 1816, providing a definitive architectural guide for the use of builders.

The most interesting thing about the Greek Revival was that it was, in reality, a romantic movement in classic garb. Greek detail was applied as a formula with varying degrees of authenticity, lacking the delicacy of the earlier Federal work which had been executed by hand. It achieved bold effects with broad, flat surfaces, monumental porticos and colonnades, and a multiplicity of readily duplicated details, made possible by the introduction of steam-operated machinery. The low, triangular pediment, with or without acroteria, was its hallmark.

It was here for the first time that asymmetry occasionally crept into the house plan, although, where a front door was set to one side, it was usually well hidden behind a symmetrical, classical portico. The germs of romantic planning were present, and the interiors often produced novel features. There was much confusion of thinking, as seen in early studies for the Subtreasury Building,† where the architect's design introduced a Roman dome into the middle of a Greek temple (its vestigial remains may be seen today in the central rotunda of that building, although the dome was never built).

The Greek Revival, which had been foreshadowed by Latrobe's Bank of Pennsylvania of 1798, in Philadelphia, did not die a sudden death but straggled along until the eighteen-fifties. With Addison Hutton's Ridgway Library of 1875, in Philadelphia, came its ultimate swan song.

Among the New York examples of Greek Revival architecture, the old Merchants' Exchange Building on Wall Street‡ is the most magnificent in its huge proportions, while Brooklyn's little Borough Hall is perhaps the most typical. Saint Peter's Church, on Barclay Street, typifies the temple form, which was also used for country houses; while the typical Greek Revival row house may best be seen along the north side of Washington Square. Sailor's Snug Harbor, on Staten Island, almost contemporary with Girard College in Philadelphia, was an entire complex of buildings and probably New York's most ambitious project carried out in the Grecian mode.

The foremost exponents of the Greek Revival in New York were Ithiel Town and his partner Alexander Jackson Davis — not to mention Minard Lafever, of Brooklyn, whose book *The Beauties of Modern Architecture* was replete with Greek details, many of which can be found in the sedate, older mansions of Brooklyn Heights. Isaiah Rogers will always be remembered for the old Merchants' Exchange and Martin E. Thompson for Sailors' Snug Harbor.

* 1821–1832.

† At northeast corner of Nassau and Wall streets (Federal Hall National Memorial).

‡ First National City Bank (previously, U.S. Customs House).

Classic Revival

The Classic Revival should be considered here, as it is a term which is often used and which, nominally at least, includes the Greek Revival.

It should include those classical buildings erected after 1830 and before the emergence of the Renaissance styles, such as the Italianate and the French Second Empire. However, it need not include the Greek Revival, as this is such a clearly defined style that it stands in its own right and tends to supersede and negate such a loose term as "Classic Revival." This leaves us with those classical buildings which are not Greek Revival, narrowing the field to structures of Roman inspiration.

There are only a few buildings remaining in New York which might be called Roman from this early period. Thomas Jefferson was the great exponent of the Roman in architecture, and his red-brick, domed Monticello and University of Virginia are typical of this American version of the Roman. He also designed the State Capitol at Richmond, Virginia, as a copy of a Roman temple.

Gothic Revival

The Gothic Revival did not represent a new national style, as it arrived more or less simultaneously with a varied assortment of revival styles. These included the Italianate or Italian villa style of architecture, the Egyptian, the Moorish, and several other less important romantic styles.

There was a new interest in the exotic and a genuine desire to explore the possibilities of the free, or asymmetrical, plan which all of these styles of architecture made possible. Heretofore, the plan had been generally symmetrical, with all its parts disposed about a central axis. Now, at last, a new freedom was introduced, both in plan and in the massing of vertical elements.

Towers, balconies, loggias, and other external manifestations appeared in profusion, while the internal arrangement of the plan achieved a dynamic quality wherein hexagonal rooms were ingeniously linked to circular, square, or rectangular chambers. Wings projected out from the central core at angles which best suited the topography or the whims of the owners. An architectural revolution had taken place.

The principal factor responsible for the introduction of the Gothic Revival to this country was literary. This influence came primarily from England, where the novels of Walter Scott and others were introducing the romantic glamor of a world of chivalry. The newly rich of the Industrial Revolution sought, in their private lives, an escape into a world of fancied mediaeval gallantry where armorial crests might be blazoned forth over porte-cocheres while pseudo-battlements and machicolations adorned the uppermost profiles of their new villas.

Closer to home, we had interpreters of this new-found English romanticism, not least of whom was Andrew Jackson Downing, the American-born Hudson River aesthete and landscape gardener. He managed, with the aid of architects newly arrived from England, to create Gothic fantasies to meet the demands of the most exacting clients. His houses were designed as adjuncts to the romantic landscapes he had created for them.

In 1842 he published his *Cottage Residences; or a Series of Designs for Rural Cottages and Cottage Villas, and Their Gardens and Grounds Adapted to North America.* Perhaps even more specific, and fairly well known in this country, was Loudon's book *An Encyclopaedia of Cottage, Farm, and Villa Architecture and Furniture* . . . sold in London as early as 1835.

In New York, Gothic fantasies took shape primarily in the form of town houses, churches, and academic buildings. One of the earliest was the West Building of the General Theological Seminary, built about 1835 and still standing on the grounds today, although the similar East Building was razed many years ago. Alexander J. Davis produced some of the most nearly perfect and original Gothic buildings in and about New York.

The Gothic Revival extended roughly from 1845 to 1860, with the Twenty-fifth Street gate of Green-Wood Cemetery in Brooklyn, of 1861, representing its culmination. In the ecclesiastical field, Gothic Revival churches continued to be built up to about 1870, when the new Victorian Gothic style superseded it.

Trinity Church at Wall Street and Saint Patrick's Cathedral on upper Fifth Avenue are the monuments of the Gothic Revival, with a host of smaller churches also representative of this style. One of the very finest of these small churches is Grace Church at East Tenth Street and Broadway. The most typical Gothic town house stands, intact, at 131 Hicks Street in Brooklyn.

The Civil War dealt the final blow to the romantic revival styles and ushered in a new, less individualistic architecture derived from Second Empire Paris.

Italianate

Roughly parallel with the development of the Gothic Revival was the equally strong revival of Italian Renaissance architecture. It was of great importance in New York as it sired the "brownstone" and the suburban "Hudson River Bracketed" house. The country version of this style was the so-called "Tuscan villa," with or without brackets under the eaves, but having almost invariably a high, square tower. This style was characterized by the asymmetrical plan, low-pitched roofs, balconies, and loggias. Its ancestor was, of course, the Roman country villa as developed and modified by the Italian Renaissance. These villas were once to be found in the outlying boroughs, but few survive today.

Here again the inspiration was literary, as in the Gothic Revival, but the influence was more nearly first-hand as travelers had brought back glowing accounts of the glories of Italy and its Renaissance architecture which were published in architectural handbooks in this country, including even such popular vehicles as *Godey's Lady's Book* magazine.

As early as 1840, James Bogardus on a trip to Italy was inspired by "the rich architectural designs of antiquity"* and determined to use them as a point of departure in the design of the cast-iron mercantile buildings he was planning to build.

* J. W. Thomson, *Cast Iron Buildings*. New York, Harrison, 1856.

In 1853, M. Field in the preface to his *City Architecture* became quite specific when he said: 'The Italian, now the fashionable style for city edifices, was the peculiar taste of the author, derived from a professional tour of the continent of Europe, long before it had superseded the pure Greek style; which however beautiful in itself, has been proved by experience to be unproductive of any original combinations, and ill adapted to modern uses and requirements." His book was profusely illustrated with designs for stores, mansions, and hotels. Similar versions may be seen in New York today, executed in brownstone with only very minor modifications.

The "brownstone," which covered block after block above Fourteenth Street in endless rows, was often built by the speculative builder without benefit of architect, once the prototype had been established. It transformed a city of brick and wood into a dull monochrome of brown elegance. Mass production was now the order of the day, and architects Vaux, Sloan, and Hobbs illustrated their books on architecture with various styles of Italian villas suitable for country residence.

The Italianate period extended roughly from 1845 to 1860 and included all types of buildings. The best examples of the "brownstone" town house are to be found on Brooklyn Heights. The Sun Building, built piecemeal by A. T. Stewart as his first great store on Chambers Street, was a fine example of early mercantile architecture. Churches such as Beecher's Plymouth Church of the Pilgrims in Brooklyn and the Friends' Meeting House at 144 East Twentieth Street at Gramercy Park were typical of the style, although lacking the campaniles of their Italian forebears. A fine example of the suburban villa may be seen in the great Litchfield Mansion located in Prospect Park, Brooklyn. It was designed by A. J. Davis.

French Influence (Second Empire)

Although it was not a revival style, chronologically the mansard-roofed architecture introduced from France belongs to the period between the Italianate, which was a revival style, and the Romanesque Revival. The word "Mansardic" has been coined to describe this style, but we hesitate to use it as it might seem to refer to the work of Jules Hardouin Mansart (1645–1708), which belonged to an earlier period of French history.

At the close of the Civil War, in 1865, a new spirit was in the air; new fortunes had emerged and, particularly in the South, old ones had gone into eclipse. It was the era of the newly rich, and it sought a new expression. It found inspiration for its architecture not in literature but in the splendid trappings of the contemporary French court. Napoleon III and his glamorous wife Eugénie were setting the pace abroad, and our parvenus were won over by the elegance of the French Second Empire.

This style was characterized by the formal, urban architecture of Baron Haussmann's Paris, of which the Paris Opera House was the resplendent star. It was an architecture characterized by mansard roofs, broken pediments, coupled columns, round or segmental arched windows, and the integral use of sculpture. Dormer windows often became oval, and roofs were crowned with iron crestings in the form of low, spiky railings. The tower remained a conspicuous feature of the country house.

This period extended from about 1865 to 1873, when the great secondary post–Civil War depression curtailed building operations. The largest single building erected in this style in New York was the old Post Office at the lower end of City Hall Park — razed some years ago — which echoed somewhat grotesquely the glories of Second Empire Paris. The American Jockey Club, now the Manhattan Club, at the northeast corner of Madison Square, is one of the finest remaining examples of this style.

The French Second Empire style did not grow out of the Italianate style but came to us from Paris. However, the two styles had many similarities, as they both ultimately found their roots in the Italian Renaissance.* The French version was always more fussy in its details and often hard to distinguish in the case of the town house.

The mansard roof invariably supplanted the cornice or roof balustrade of the Italianate. In its country or suburban version, the French often retained the main lines of the Italian villa, with the addition of the high mansard roof and iron crestings. The exterior walls were generally shorn of miscellaneous balconies and loggias, while in the more pretentious houses, the porte-cochere was the most conspicuous addition. The new feeling was one of cold elegance, with a new emphasis on symmetry, as opposed to the playful asymmetry of its predecessor. An architecture which sought similarity and conformity had taken the place of one which expressed a capricious individuality.

Romanesque Revival

The last of the revival styles was the Romanesque Revival. The buildings which were built in this style were often referred to as "Richardsonian Romanesque," named after Henry Hobson Richardson (1838–1886), the great Boston architect who was so influential in establishing it here in the United States.

The Romanesque Revival may be roughly divided into two phases. The first phase extended from about 1845 to 1870 and included a very naïve version of Romanesque architecture, paralleling the true revival styles.† The second phase began in 1870, shortly after Richardson's return from France, where he had been studying at the Ecole des Beaux Arts in Paris. It extended up to about 1893, when it was almost superseded by the classical influence of the World's Columbian Exposition at Chicago.

The buildings of the first phase, of which few examples remain to us, were generally executed in brick with round arched openings and a profusion of exterior pilasters and roof corbels. Low-pitched gables were often introduced, and this style was commonly used for commercial buildings, armories, private stables, and other utilitarian buildings.

* Henry-Russell Hitchcock has advanced the theory that this style did not come to us directly from Paris but via England, where the great hotels and commercial buildings, influenced by the French Second Empire, were the models which were passed down to us. See Henry-Russell Hitchcock, Jr., *The Architecture of H. H. Richardson and His Times* (New York, Museum of Modern Art, 1936), p. 16.

† C. L. V. Meeks, "Romanesque Before Richardson." *Art Bulletin*, Vol. 35, p. 21.

The Marble Collegiate Church at Fifth Avenue and Twenty-ninth Street, built in 1851, is a good example. The first example of Romanesque Revival architecture in New York was the Church of the Pilgrims* at the corner of Henry and Remsen streets in Brooklyn, designed by Richard Upjohn in 1844, although infinitely superior as architecture to other examples of the first phase.

In one sense, the second or Richardsonian phase of the Romanesque Revival was no more a revival than the French Second Empire architecture which we had borrowed from Paris. Richardson, who introduced it, brought to this country the fruits of his Parisian experience in the form of an architecture which, although it had been revived in France, was being practiced as a contemporary style.

Although Richardson's work at the Ecole was conservative and conformed largely to Classical and Renaissance canons of taste, it must be remembered that a new ferment of rebellion was in the air. The archaeologist Viollet-le-Duc had already introduced his regenerated mediaevalism to the Ecole, while exponents of the Romanesque were currently doing their school *projets* in this style. It is certain that these new forces, tending toward the revival of mediaevalism in architecture, had their deep and lasting influence on Richardson and became his principal mode of expression soon after his return to the United States in 1865.

The Romanesque Revival in this country was exemplified by a masonry bearing wall tradition. In its quest for an honest expression, it sedulously avoided the use of iron lintels — thus leading directly to its outstanding characteristic, the masonry arch. Large openings were often spanned by arches, while smaller openings, which could be spanned by stone lintels, were often square-headed. At its best, the use of materials was highly expressive and often decorative, where an incised ornament or stones of variegated colors were used. The color scheme was important, with dark colors generally favored. Door and window frames were made to harmonize with the somber tone of the masonry and were often painted dark brown or green with sash of dark red.

Many small buildings of this style were executed in wood, with shingle roofs and walls. Quite illogically, they often retained the circular towers and arches reminiscent of the stone buildings from which they derived, and they may well be placed within Vincent Scully's broadly inclusive designation, the "Shingle Style."†

Of the second or Richardsonian phase of Romanesque Revival architecture, we unfortunately have no notable examples of Richardson's own work in New York. However, he had quite a few admirers and followers here who carried out projects in this style with varying degrees of competence.

One of the finest examples in Manhattan is the south wing of the American Museum of Natural History on Seventy-seventh Street, while the DeVinne Press Building on Lafayette Street represents a more individualized interpretation of the style.

* Not to be confused with Henry Ward Beecher's Plymouth Church of the Pilgrims on Orange Street.

† Vincent Scully, Jr., *The Shingle Style.* New Haven, Yale University Press, 1955.

Brooklyn, of all the boroughs, has probably the greatest number of Romanesque Revival buildings. From the masterful hand of Frank Freeman we have the old Brooklyn Fire Headquarters, several fine residences, and a hotel. The Franklin Trust, on Montague Street, is a good example of the Romanesque "skyscraper," while the Charles Millard Pratt residence, on Clinton Avenue, best exemplifies this style in the field of domestic architecture.

The Romanesque Revival led nowhere, but it brought to this country an awareness of the expressive use of fine materials. Belonging to the masonry tradition, with the advent of steel construction it was left in a stagnant backwater, although Frank Freeman tried to bridge this gap with his radical design for the Hotel Margaret on Brooklyn Heights.

Other Revival Styles

Among revival styles prior to 1850 there were several which never won general acceptance and which were never built to any great extent. They did, however, leave a few examples in their wake.

One of these was the *Egyptian Revival,* about which Frank J. Roos, Jr., has written so well.* This style had the potential of becoming a national style like the Greek Revival, yet there were complexities which actually prevented its use from becoming widespread. First, there was the inappropriateness of the symbolism to our Christian world; secondly, the difficulty of introducing windows; and finally, the requirement that many of the exterior walls be battered.

Despite the fact that it came to us via France, through our interest in Napoleon's campaign in Egypt, there were many who resisted it. One amusing critic who went so far as to attack it vehemently on religious grounds said: "Egyptian architecture reminds us of the religion which called it into being, the most degraded and revolting paganism which ever existed. It is the architecture of embalmed cats and deified crocodiles."†

In New York, the old Tombs prison, which once stood between Franklin and Leonard streets fronting on Center Street, was probably the outstanding monument of the Egyptian Revival in this country, with the possible exception of certain prisons in other states. The cemetery was one of the few places where it was apparently considered appropriate, probably due to its association with death. New Haven and Newport both boasted Egyptian cemetery gates. In Brooklyn's Green-Wood Cemetery, one treasure of this unique style remains to us today — the tomb of Dr. James Anderson on Cliff Path, Sylvan Cliff, overlooking Sylvan Water.

In rural areas, including the boroughs outside of Manhattan, and especially on Staten Island, a multiplicity of country villas were constructed, including the revivals already discussed. In addition to these, the handbooks of the day extolled the beauties of Anglo-Norman, Elizabethan, Venetian, Moorish, and plain ordinary Suburban Villas. None of these styles ever achieved the proportions of a revival. They simply co-existed with the revival styles, and few are left today, in their original condition, to tell the story.

* Frank J. Roos, Jr., "The Egyptian Style." *Magazine of Art,* Vol. 33, April 1940.

† Unsigned article, *North American Review,* Vol. 43, 1836.

A transitional period, which Wayne Andrews has fittingly named the "Age of Inde-cision,"* was that period after the Civil War during which we were trying to find our way. We were seeking a new style — not necessarily a national style, but one which would be suited to our way of life. This quest was being carried on simultaneously with the flowering of the popular French Second Empire style which had swept the country and was so easily re-produced by the jerry-builders and carpenters throughout the land.

It was during this period that we essayed, in our urban architecture, the Neo-Grec and the Victorian Gothic, both of which were killed by the depression which began in 1873. Minor currents of the 'seventies were to be found in the influence of Sir Charles Locke Eastlake's "honest furniture,"† in which every leg, joint, bracket, and shelf loudly pro-claimed its function. All of this found its way into a weird assortment of summer houses, cottages, boathouses, and other minor structures for which no porch could be built without innumerable braces, brackets, and similar superfluous connections. The walls were usually covered with an ill-assorted veneer of notched vertical battens and pseudo-timbering, pro-ducing the general effect of a Swiss chalet.

Later, during the 'eighties, we toyed with the versatile Queen Anne style, or the "free classic," as it has been so aptly named. It is interesting to note that these sincere though abortive efforts were being made by the architects, as they were dissatisfied with the French "formula" which had proven so popular with the jerry-builders and the general public.

Neo-Grec

The Neo-Grec style must not in any way be confused with the Greek Revival, al-though it employed a greatly simplified version of Greek ornament, "modernized" to suit the demands of brick, stone, and cast iron. In this country it had a short life, lasting only from 1860 to about 1873.

Again, the influence for this style came from Paris and the Ecole des Beaux Arts. The French architect Henri Labrouste was the foremost exponent of the Neo-Grec and advo-cated the free combination of wrought iron and stone. Most of his work was being done in the 1840's, although the Neo-Grec did not reach these shores until Richard Morris Hunt returned from his studies in Paris in 1855. Hunt did not execute anything of note in this style in New York until considerably later. The Tribune Building on Printing House Square, near City Hall, is basically a Neo-Grec building, although it combines with it a Ruskinian polychromy and certain mediaeval details.

Most notable features of this style are long, parallel, incised lines on pilasters, usually set too far apart to be confused with fluting; use of acroteria at the ends of pediments, so simplified that they are usually just blocks of stone cocked slightly upward and outward; incised, single-line ornament very much stylized in execution; circular escutcheons or

* Wayne Andrews, *Architecture, Ambition and Americans.* New York, Harper & Brothers, 1947.

† Charles L. Eastlake, *Hints on Household Taste.* English and American editions, 1868–1883.

medallions introduced into entablatures above columns and Ionic capitals, similar to those used in the interior of the Temple of Apollo Epicurus at Bassae. When used in cast-iron buildings for square columns between windows, the Neo-Grec influence can usually be detected, as only the side facing the street is profiled and moulded, while the sides adjoining the windows are absolutely flat. Sometimes in masonry buildings the process is reversed for door and window frames where the flat face is toward the street while the outer edges of the frame are elaborately profiled.

We find in the Neo-Grec an attempt to reconcile classic detail with "modern" construction of stone or iron where the attenuation of structural members had become a determining factor. Montgomery Schuyler, who wrote about it more extensively than any of the other contemporary critics, said: "It professed to offer the reconciliation of the classicism of the schools with the new romantic impulse."* Today, we can see an example of this style in the cast-iron building designed by Hunt at 480 Broadway. The old Lenox Library which stood on the site of the Frick Museum, and the base of the Statue of Liberty, were probably Hunt's finest exemplifications of the Neo-Grec.

Victorian Gothic

As its name implies, Victorian Gothic architecture stems from the Gothic tradition, with emphasis on Italian Gothic.† This is so much the case that it is often referred to as "Venetian Gothic." However, due to the heterogeneity of elements which may be found expressed in it, the all-inclusive name Victorian Gothic is a better designation. In New York, it covered the period from about 1860 to 1880.

Within this tradition, we find several influences at work, all of which stem from Gothic architecture. Perhaps the primary influence was polychromy, deriving from Ruskin's studies of the Italian Gothic. His *Stones of Venice*, first published in 1851, appeared in the United States at the same time and had a wide influence over the years. The secondary influence was that stemming from Viollet-le-Duc's archaeological studies of Gothic architecture, which appeared as the *Dictionnaire Raisonné de l'Architecture* in ten volumes, published between the years 1854 and 1868. Viollet-le-Duc's influence introduced primarily strains of twelfth- and thirteenth-century French Gothic.

Naturally, these influences found their first repercussions in England, where Burges, Street, Waterhouse, and Butterfield all produced, at various times, an architecture which might be described as primarily Ruskinian. Ruskin's Oxford Museum, designed in collaboration with the architect Woodward in 1859, served as a prototype for much Victorian Gothic work. The Albert Memorial of 1872, by Sir George Gilbert Scott, set a great vogue in high elaboration, although it was never widely influential here.

Our first notable structure in this style was actually Venetian Gothic and reminiscent

* Montgomery Schuyler, "A Review of the Works of Richard Morris Hunt." *Architectural Record*, Vol. V, No. 2, October–December 1895.

† Montgomery Schuyler, "Italian Gothic in New York." *Architectural Record*, Vol. XXVI, No. 1, July 1909.

of the Doge's Palace in Venice. It was designed by Peter B. Wight in 1862 for the National Academy of Design, and it stood at the northwest corner of East Twenty-third Street and Fourth Avenue.

Richard Morris Hunt was very much influenced by the work of Viollet-le-Duc, and his Stuyvesant Apartment, which once stood on East Eighteenth Street, was largely affected by the early French Gothic tradition.

Today we have the Jefferson Market Courthouse, at the corner of West Tenth Street and Sixth Avenue, as not only a fine example of high Victorian Gothic, but also as a superb example of town planning, tailor-made for its site. It was designed in 1875 by architects Withers and Vaux, both of whom had come to America from England.

Victorian Gothic architecture was costly to build and belonged to a richly decorated masonry tradition which rarely found its way into the domestic field. It was usually employed in the construction of churches and public buildings. It vanished, as a style, during the secondary post–Civil War depression, which began in 1873, although Victorian Gothic buildings continued to appear sporadically for many years, particularly in the small outlying towns.

Queen Anne

A fashion of fashions, sometimes referred to as the bric-à-brac style — the Queen Anne, as it became known — was not an attempt to establish a national style. It was borrowed from England, and its quaint interiors and picturesque profiles spread quickly throughout a nation in search of a cozy domesticity. It ran its course parallel to the Romanesque Revival and was also more or less killed by the classicism of the World's Columbian Exposition. Although it derives its name from Queen Anne, it owes hardly anything to that period of pre-Georgian English architecture. It comes much closer to the half-timbered manor house of Elizabethan times, modified by Flemish and Classic detail. It is for this reason that it is often referred to as the "Free Classic," since the orders as we know them were abandoned, and in their place a hodgepodge of Classic details was introduced.

In its country version, it may well be grouped with our "Shingle Style" houses; while its urban version, generally executed in brick, tended toward the Flemish, with arched or stepped gable ends, chimneys replete with slender pilasters signalizing the flues within, and copper or wood bay windows subdivided by a multiplicity of muntins.

The principal advocate of the Queen Anne style in England was Richard Norman Shaw (1831–1912),* a scholarly architect who sought to evolve a livable style suited to the needs of English life. That he did so with his own peculiar hybrid style, in which he wed the Flemish to the Elizabethan, may be one of the reasons why this new architecture was so often unsuccessfully executed by uninspired followers.

In the 1870's a certain interest was reawakened in our "colonial" heritage, and in

* Walter Knight Sturges, "The Long Shadow of Norman Shaw." *Journal of the Society of Architectural Historians,* Vol. IX, No. 4, December 1950.

country houses a sort of attenuated Georgian was added to the potpourri that was the Queen Anne. The color scheme, as in Romanesque Revival, was somber, running to reds and greens, while pressed brick with thin black mortar joints often combined with scalloped red shingles and panels displaying sunbursts and the ubiquitous sunflower motif.*

In New York, we have few examples of this style worthy of comment; however, the old Gorham Company Building, at the northwest corner of Broadway and East Nineteenth Street, exemplifies the large brick commercial building.

Montgomery Schuyler deplored this sterile attempt to return to a past domesticity when he said: "In an evil hour, and under a strange spell, the young architects of the United States followed the young architects of England in preferring the refinements of a fixed and developed architecture to the rudeness of a living and growing architecture."†

The Queen Anne was an architectural exercise in virtuosity, played on an old theme. Because of its emphasis on the superficial treatment of surfaces, it made little contribution in the realm of plan or structure.

ECLECTICISM (GENERAL)

In the world of philosophy, the word "eclecticism" is used to describe a system of thought which has borrowed various elements from existing known philosophies to create something new. Theoretically, eclecticism in architecture would describe an architecture in which many elements from different architectures have been combined to create a new building — however, common usage, the literature of architecture, and a study of architectural history prove that such is not the case. An eclectic — that is, an architect who practices eclecticism — is one who borrows freely from various past styles of architecture but who generally uses only one style for a given building.‡

This concept of borrowing styles to create a new architecture existed in the various revival styles we have reviewed, but there is a very important difference between that type of borrowing and the eclectic borrowing which began soon after the World's Columbian Exposition.

Revival styles were usually movements of nationwide import, lasting for a given period of time and generally executed by architects who worked primarily in a particular style of architecture while it lasted. There was a naïve spontaneity expressed in these movements which set them apart from other movements and often evoked the strongest expressions of partisanship from their proponents. Talbot Hamlin has remarked that there was

* *Modern Architectural Designs and Details . . . Showing New and Original Designs in the Queen Anne . . .* New York, William T. Comstock, 1881.

† Montgomery Schuyler, *American Architecture: Concerning the Queen Anne.* New York, Harper & Brothers, 1892.

‡ The chief exception to this observation is the case where interiors of different periods or styles are introduced into a building which, seen from the street, presents on the exterior a uniform style of architecture.

"a kind of simple motivation, quite different from the self-conscious choosing of style that we usually deem an integral part of eclecticism."*

The eclecticism which began after the Chicago Fair of 1893 was a highly self-conscious process in which the creation of architecture became a sort of shopping for styles, where the architect was the buyer and the one who through his purchases set the styles. After the Fair there was a great resurgence of classicism, ranging from the wildest Renaissance creations to the most conservative and academically correct Roman examples. As the dream of the "Great White City" faded from memory, a host of other styles were introduced into the architectural world, under the aegis of an architecturally correct eclecticism.

Although an eclectic architect would not usually combine several styles in one building, he might use different styles for several buildings he was designing simultaneously.

The two factors which contributed most to the development and spread of eclecticism were the book and the concomitant development of photography as a medium for the illustration of books. These were the tools of the serious student of architecture; they made possible a high degree of selectivity from a broad range of world architectures.

We made great strides in one direction, unaware that the price we paid was the almost complete annihilation of the vernacular tradition, the native, the indigenous, and any possibility of their development. There are many who believe that there is such a thing as creative eclecticism, and undoubtedly we did eventually evolve an architecture which was expressive of our way of life and our native materials. It seems, in retrospect, that the eclectic approach to the study of architecture, although it produced many monuments, did not particularly assist or encourage creative processes of thought.

A few rebels like Frank Lloyd Wright, Louis Sullivan, and others of the Chicago School emancipated their thought processes from preconceived ideas and from the need of borrowing from past cultures. They believed in solving each problem as though it were completely new, relying solely on the terms of its requirements. They did evolve a new school of thought, a new way of planning, and even a new ornament; all were creative contributions to our native culture, although they had little influence in New York.

The study of eclecticism — what it was, what forces lay behind it, and why it developed — raises some of the most fascinating enigmas of our architectural history. Countless theories have been advanced, and we hear of symbolic eclecticism, synthetic eclecticism, and creative eclecticism† — all variants on the eclectic theme and worthy of investigation. Here we must limit ourselves to only the most rudimentary explanation of what it was and how it affected our architectural development.

The World's Columbian Exposition at Chicago, in 1893, provided a new challenge to the American mentality. The ragged, toothless appearance of "Middletown" had been superseded by a vision, the vision of the Great White City. Those who saw the lagoon by moon-

* Talbot F. Hamlin, "The Rise of Eclecticism in New York." *Journal of the Society of Architectural Historians,* Vol. 11, No. 2, May 1952, p. 3.

† Carroll L. V. Meeks, "Creative Eclecticism." *Journal of the Society of Architectural Historians,* Vol. 12, No. 4, December 1953.

light carried back memories of a fairy city — of what a city might be. It stimulated their ambitions to create the City Beautiful in place of the mean ugliness of Main Street. The money was there, the technology at hand, and it only remained to reproduce the vision, however misguided the concept.

That this order and beauty came to us solely in the guise of a Classic Renaissance was a misfortune insofar as the broad development of our architecture was concerned; the gain was made in the realm of town planning, where a comprehensive unity had been achieved. The uniform cornice line which was established around the Lagoon at the Fair was, in itself, a first-hand experience in orderliness for those who saw it. It represented a new discipline in design — that which had created Paris, a city which few Americans had ever seen.

The influence of the Eastern architects, headed by Richard Morris Hunt, prevailed in dictating the uniform classicism of the major buildings at the Fair; and the Western architects, led by D. H. Burnham, took up the battle cry. After the Fair, the great wave of classicism which swept the country was a new order instituted by the architects and carefully controlled by their canons of taste.

McKim, Mead & White in the East and Daniel H. Burnham in the West found themselves, almost overnight, faced with the problem of establishing a new classic architecture on a nationwide scale. This new architecture would require the most costly materials and the finest detail. It was a game which had to be played according to the rules; the very use of the architectural orders required that. The proportioning and detailing of a colonnade could not be a hit-or-miss affair; it must be derived from the finest examples, based on European precedent.

Armies of draftsmen had to be trained in the proper use of the classic orders. They had to be able to translate literally the architect's little pencil sketch into a complete working drawing, from which the building might be built, true in every proportion and using only the appropriate ornament. Out of all this grew the wholesale shipment of young men to Paris to study at the Ecole des Beaux Arts and, at a later date, to Rome to study the glories of the Eternal City. Subsidies and fellowships were forthcoming to train a generation of architects, and both McKim and Burnham fought to raise the necessary money to establish the American Academy in Rome.

The Paris school produced a highly sophisticated version of Renaissance architecture, while Rome taught a purer classic style for which a scholarly knowledge of the orders was a primary requisite. The architectural schools in this country were called upon to maintain a high level of architectural excellence, a knowledge of precedent derived from books, and, where possible, a first-hand acquaintance with the examples of antiquity.

Edith Wharton, a keen observer of the formative influences which produced the civilization of her time, noted that young men were beginning to take up architecture and even archaeology as professions in addition to the time-honored careers in the law and business. She sensed the forces at work which produced this change when she pointed out that "with the coming of the new millionaires the building of big houses had begun, in

New York and in the country, bringing with it a keen interest in architecture, furniture and works of art in general. . . . Several of the younger architects were acquiring the important professional libraries which have been one of the chief elements in forming American taste in architecture."*

The era of the architect had dawned; gone was the builder-architect and the age of revivals. The demands of ever larger commissions, involving the coordination of many trades and professions, required that the architect take the lead role. He was forced to meet the ever accelerating tempo of the times, to be able to produce large commissions on short notice, in a highly competitive world, with a high degree of competence. He needed a ready formula to enable him to fly quickly into action, and he needed a staff capable of translating his schemes onto paper, from which the steel, bricks, and mortar might be interpreted into reality.

Eclecticism gave the architect a working basis on which to proceed. It was not primarily creative, it was assimilative, derived almost invariably from precedent adapted to meet a new set of conditions. This required great ingenuity but tended to produce a stereotyped world availing itself of an industrialized economy where mass production made possible the end result. We see this end result in the temple-banks of the early nineteen-hundreds, in the repetitive use of limestone and yellow brick, and in the white trim of a singularly sterile period.

The glass and steel so boldly deployed in French Beaux Arts buildings found here a timid reproduction. Except for such gifted men as Ernest Flagg and a few others who had been trained in Paris, the lesson was lost. Our neo-classicism foundered in a repetitive maze of classical orders and masonry walls, while the great contribution of French intellect, which might have led us onward, was lost to our chosen mediocrity.

Eclecticism may be said to have begun in 1893† and to have died toward the end of the nineteen-twenties, when our architects began to evolve an expressive architecture of their own. The great economic forces shaping our lives were the forces which, with the advent of the skyscraper and the high-rise apartment, brought us to the realization that if our architects did not evolve a radical new design, the engineers would.

The various styles followed by the word "eclectic," to which we shall refer hereafter, may be readily placed in the chronological scale of architectural development following the Chicago Fair. Perhaps we are now more aware of that strange confluence of forces which led us so suddenly into the eclectic phase of our development.

CLASSIC STYLES

As we have seen, the great resurgence of classic architecture began in 1893. It was sponsored by the architects and included all phases of classicism.

* Edith Wharton, *A Backward Glance* (New York, D. Appleton-Century Co., Inc., 1934), p. 148.

† Thomas E. Talmadge, *The Story of Architecture in America*. New York, W. W. Norton, 1927. (See esp. Chapter X.)

Georgian Eclectic

Georgian architecture is considered by many to be a survival architecture having a continuous tradition. Actually, between colonial times and the eighteen-seventies, when an interest in it began to reawaken, there was a period when it was not a living architecture at all. After 1893 it again came into its own, along with the other more elaborate phases of classicism. It was executed with the scholarly correctness of the other eclectic styles and was often derived from the English originals. The old portion of the Harvard Club on West Fourty-fourth Street, designed by McKim, Mead & White, is a fine example of this style.

Federal Eclectic

This one-time national style of the young Republic did not re-emerge with the post-Fair classicism at once, but only after 1900. In the 'twenties it became particularly popular as a sort of veneer for the large, new apartment houses and hotels which sprang up all over the city shortly before the financial crash of 1929. As used at this time, it was replete with Adamesque detail and was also particularly favored for city residences and large country houses. John Russell Pope and Delano & Aldrich were among its most ardent proponents.

Roman Eclectic

The style of architecture most revered by the eclectic architects, for the propagation of which the American Academy in Rome was founded, was classic Roman architecture. No bank was considered respectable, after 1893, if it could not boast a temple front, or at least a Doric colonnade. Pennsylvania Station represented the epitome of the Roman in New York. The main waiting room of the station was reminiscent of the Baths of Caracalla in Rome. Some of McKim, Mead & White's buildings, and Welles Bosworth's American Telephone and Telegraph Building, re-created the classic grandeur of Rome in New York in structures where the very height of the orders was awe-inspiring.

Beaux Arts Eclectic

The Ecole des Beaux Arts in Paris trained a generation of architects in the rather free French interpretation of classic architecture. It ranged from such almost Roman types as Cass Gilbert's U.S. Government Custom House at Bowling Green to the more typically French interpretations of classicism, such as the New York Public Library by Carrère & Hastings and the south façade of Grand Central Station designed by Whitney Warren, where the large areas of steel and glass usually associated with the French version of classicism were much in evidence.

Classic Eclectic

This is the all-inclusive term which may be said to include the Roman and the Beaux

Arts Eclectic; however, it is too all-inclusive to give any idea of the actual style designated. In our Index of Buildings it has been used to designate structures such as Bruce Price's American Surety Building on lower Broadway, which vaunts a handsome Greek Ionic colonnade at the first floor while Beaux Arts sculptured figures flank oval windows at the upper stories. It could also be used to describe Greek buildings of the Eclectic period and any other classic buildings which are not either specifically Roman or Beaux Arts.

Renaissance Eclectic

This, again, is such an all-inclusive designation that it is almost useless when we have such clear designations as "Italian Renaissance Eclectic," "French Renaissance Eclectic," and many others. It is used here only to designate those Renaissance buildings which, for one reason or another, do not fall under any of the Renaissance styles mentioned below.

Italian Renaissance Eclectic

This is a style which was very much favored by the leading eclectic architects, as it was sanctified by having been taught at the American Academy in Rome. The Racquet and Tennis Club on Park Avenue, by McKim, Mead & White, is a fine example; and the Judson Memorial Church on Washington Square South, by the same firm, is another.

French Renaissance Eclectic

Here we must make a careful distinction between the early French Renaissance architecture of François I — the chateaux of the Loire Valley, which belong to this style — and the later French styles erected during the reign of Louis XIII through that of Louis XVI, which, although they were actually a continuation of the French Renaissance, were usually designated in this country by the King Louis whose reign coincided with the period.

The French Renaissance is best typified in New York by the Felix Warburg house at East Ninety-second Street and Fifth Avenue, and by the ornament on the Alwyn Court Apartments on Seventh Avenue.

French Classic Eclectic

The styles which are included in the French Classic Eclectic are those which come under the reign of Louis XIII through that of the ill-fated Louis XVI. Everything represented here led ultimately into that later and freer version of French Classic architecture, the Beaux Arts Eclectic. There was a delicacy and charm to be found in this French style which was often lacking in contemporary versions in other countries. One of the best examples in New York of the earliest period, the Louis XIII period, is the Miller house at the southeast corner of Fifth Avenue and East Eighty-sixth Street. Of the latest period, that of Louis XVI, a good example is the Frick Museum on Fifth Avenue at East Seventieth Street. The American interpretation was often coarse and overly heavy; however, New York City does have some of the finest examples in the country. Horace Trumbauer's Duke Mansion on Fifth Avenue, not to mention several of his superb travertine town houses, probably represent the epitome of this style in New York.

Flemish Renaissance Eclectic

The Flemish Renaissance, which so much influenced the Queen Anne style, persisted in a few examples into the eclectic period. It was, of course, carried out in a manner closer to that of the Belgian and Dutch originals, but the very nature of this ornate style permitted a wide latitude in design. The West End Collegiate Church and School at West Seventy-seventh Street and West End Avenue, by R. W. Gibson, is a good example.

German Renaissance Eclectic

The high apostle of the German Renaissance in New York was Henry Janeway Hardenbergh, who designed the Dakota Apartments. Superficially, this style, with its high roofs and chimneys, resembles the French Renaissance Eclectic. The detail is apt to be heavier, the figures in sculpture and ironwork more grotesque, while the dormers are used more profusely and gable ends are considerably more in evidence.

Romanesque Eclectic

Of all the major revival styles, the Romanesque was the most neglected by the Eclectics. Perhaps the reason was that it did not fit readily into any known formula. It was a highly individualized style in which no two buildings were alike and for which there was no set plan or ornament to be followed. The sculpture had always been the unique product of the local sculptor. York & Sawyer in New York made the style their own, and the results were invariably good. These buildings were usually executed in stone. The Bowery Savings Bank on East Forty-second Street is a good example and has a most impressive interior.

GOTHIC STYLES

The Gothic styles re-emerged in the early nineteen-hundreds, not so much as a rebellion against classicism but as a supplement to it. Their introduction filled a need in solving the problem of how best to express the high building. Piling tiers of classical orders one above the other had been essayed in the old Saint Paul Building and in the American Telephone and Telegraph Building at the lower end of City Hall Park; it had not provided a solution. The architects felt that a vertical emphasis was needed, and the soaring lines of Gothic architecture seemed to have the inherent quality desired.

Gothic Eclectic

Facing many of the problems which had been met by the architects of the Romanesque Eclectic style, those who espoused the Gothic cause succeeded, with the aid of the terra-cotta companies, in evolving a sort of formula of ornament. In this solution to the problem, trefoils, quatrefoils, ogival arches, and other details were reduced to a common denominator compatible with the skyscraper and the office building (Commercial Gothic), the church (Ecclesiastical Gothic), and the school or college (Collegiate Gothic).

Cass Gilbert won the acclaim of the city with his Woolworth Building in 1913, where the Gothic structural forms and the detail seemed well adapted to the soaring verticality of the skyscraper. Some of the churches, such as Saint Thomas's on Fifth Avenue, by Cram, Goodhue & Ferguson, were executed in stone with great attention to detail. Many others clove to the versatile terra cotta. George B. Post's City College of New York, at West 135th Street in upper Manhattan, is a good example of a large complex of buildings carried out in this style. The Venetian Gothic was also essayed by the Eclectics and is well exemplified by the Montauk Club at the Grand Army Plaza in Brooklyn.

ART NOUVEAU

In the early nineteen-hundreds the Art Nouveau style, which came to us via France and Belgium, had quite a vogue. Although its plasticity of form and freedom from convention appealed to such intelligent young architects as Robert D. Kohn and a few others, it was never widely accepted by conservative architects in this country. It was usually only in the large cities that it appeared at all. Beginning about 1905, the hardware manufacturers, following Tiffany's lead, introduced many Art Nouveau designs; and, in the realm of furniture and bric-a-brac, it did become quite popular for a short time. Robert D. Kohn's Evening Post Building on Vesey Street was a challenge to New York which, had it been understood and developed further, might have led us into a new realm of architecture.

MODERNE

The French *Exposition des Arts Decoratifs,* which was held in 1925, introduced a new decorative medium based on stylized plant and animal forms. This opened yet another door to the skyscraper architect. He was seeking an appropriate expression for his high buildings. A band of this ornament, in low relief, may be seen around the base of the Chanin Building, on the southwest corner of Lexington Avenue and East Forty-second Street; and the ceiling of the ballroom of the Waldorf-Astoria Hotel also displays some fine designs. This style of ornament was widely adopted, in the early 'twenties, for store fronts, restaurants, and cafeterias.

CONCLUSION

As our study of New York architecture ends with 1930, we might say that it is concluded with the financial crash of 1929. Up to this time the high building had been made possible through the development of the high-speed electric elevator and the fact that technological advances in both the fabrication and the erection of steel had kept pace with the new heights made possible.

The architects of high buildings were seeking an expressive medium to use as a veneer. The concept of stainless steel, glass, and aluminum lay ahead. Brick, terra cotta, and limestone were the prime building materials. Working in low relief, with only the shallowest possible breaks in wall planes, due to the fact that walls were carried on steel shelf angles supported by the steel skeleton, the architects were challenged to find a new solution for wall treatments. The deep door and window reveals of the bearing-wall masonry tradition were not expressive of the construction of the new high building.

There was, again, the quest for a national style which suggested a clean break with European precedent. Experiments were made with color, as in Raymond Hood's American Radiator Building and in the work of Ely Jacques Kahn. Voorhees, Gmelin & Walker made notable studies in the subtle gradation of brick colors and originated an ornament by which much of their work for the telephone and telegraph companies may be recognized.

Aztec* and American Indian themes were introduced; but, whatever the ornament, it soon became evident that, after we had passed twelve stories, only the base and the top of the building required special decorative treatment. The unencumbered shaft became plain, while the top, too high for finely detailed ornament to be properly seen, became largely a problem in creating an interesting profile against the sky. The base was best expressed with low-relief ornament and elaborately decorated entrances. The Chrysler Building relied on commercial symbols, while other buildings were bedizened with the weird inventions of their designers.

Architectural design in the United States has run the gamut of world styles, has originated others, and is today facing up to the stern reality of expressing structure. Probably the greatest single event in this history was the change from bearing-wall construction to the steel-skeleton-supported building. Because we had become more conscious of styles than of materials, we were not immediately aware of the implications of the change. We continued to attempt to carry ponderous walls of masonry on steel frames, simulating those with which we were familiar. It has been only since 1920 that we have introduced suitable materials and lightweight veneers into the construction of our high buildings.

The styles overawed us with their splendid externals; they prevented us from seeing the simple, expressively constructed bearing-wall structures which, because they were a fine expression of their type of construction, had style. The delusively veneered skeleton structure, whether emphasizing the vertical or the horizontal, prevented us from seeing what we had evolved in the high building. Today we are learning to express that underlying structure, and where we do so, the building has style.

* Francisco Mujica, *History of the Skyscraper*. Paris, Archaeology and Architecture Press, 1929.

DEFINITIONS OF GENERAL TERMS

Modified, as used in the Index of Buildings, implies that the basic style of the building has been changed to such an extent that this fact should be signalized.

Neo-. This prefix indicates a new version of any given style, such as Neo-Grec, Neo-Palladian, etc.

Proto-. This word, where it precedes another, implies that a building or monument so described is a prototype or predecessor of the style mentioned.

Vernacular, as used, refers to things native, or homemade. Buildings which are not of foreign origin but were constructed subject to local influences and climatic conditions might be said to be vernacular or indigenous structures.

VII. PLATES

MORRIS-JUMEL HOUSE West 160th Street and Jumel Terrace. This house is named after two notable tenants: Roger Morris, who built it, and Stephen Jumel's widow, who married Aaron Burr in his old age. The handsome Georgian interior includes an elongated eight-sided drawing room and exquisite architectural details throughout.

SAINT PAUL'S CHAPEL Broadway between Fulton and Vesey streets. This chapel, where George Washington worshiped, was designed to face the North River, with its very fine spire above the entry. The porch on Broadway provided a secondary entrance. The interior with its High Georgian detail appears today much as it did when built. It is the sole survivor of all those ancient churches which once abounded in lower Manhattan, including the Dutch Reformed Lower, Middle, and North churches; the Garden Street Church; and the Old Brick Church.

DYCKMAN HOUSE   Broadway at West 204th Street. Although the Dutch founded New York (New Amsterdam), there are few houses left to remind us of their presence. The last of the step-gabled town houses disappeared with our grandfathers, and all that remain today are a few Dutch Colonial farmhouses in Brooklyn and Queens and this reconstructed farm-house in Manhattan.

SAINT MARK'S-IN-THE-BOUWERIE   Northwest corner Stuyvesant Street and Second Avenue. Occupying what is often described as the oldest site of continuous worship in Manhattan, this church as seen today embodies a series of additions in various styles of architecture, made over a considerable period of years. The main body of the church is basically Georgian, while the steeple is Greek Revival and the cast-iron porch is Italianate.

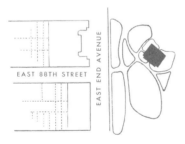

GRACIE MANSION   Carl Schurz Park, East End Avenue at East 88th Street. Built originally by Archibald Gracie, this house is beautifully situated on the East River. As the one-time home of the Museum of the City of New York, it was preserved for us; as the Mayor's house, it is well cared for today. It is probably the only one of the old country seats of Manhattan which remains a family dwelling.

ABIGAIL ADAMS SMITH HOUSE 421 East 61st Street. This building was originally a carriage house on the estate of Colonel William S. Smith, aide-de-camp to Washington and husband of Abigail Adams, the daughter of President John Adams. The estate was known as "Smith's Folly." After his failure in business, about 1800, the buildings were bought by William T. Robinson and were said to have been completed by him. In 1826 the main house burned, and in 1830 the carriage house was bought by Jeremiah Towle, remaining in the possession of his family until 1906. It was later purchased by the Colonial Dames of America, who make it their headquarters today.

MISSION OF OUR LADY OF THE ROSARY (Shrine of Blessed Elizabeth Seton) 7 State Street. When State Street was a fine residential street overlooking the Battery, the young republic was expressing itself architecturally in its new Federal style. Lightness and elegance tended to supersede the heavy richness of the Georgian town house. The fact that this façade with its airy colonnade has survived through the years is one of the miracles of Manhattan.

CHAMBERS STREET

BROADWAY

NEW YORK CITY HALL   City Hall Park. Quite aside from its position as the key governmental building of Greater New York, City Hall is an architectural treasure without peer. It was ostensibly designed by the architects Mangin and McComb, working together. However, it is now well established that this delicate creation, with its ample fenestration and curving double staircase, was principally the work of the Frenchman Joseph François Mangin.

CASTLE CLINTON NATIONAL MONUMENT   Battery Park. Originally built as one of the harbor forts that defended the entrance to the North River, it was first named Castle Clinton. It later became a roofed-in public amusement hall known as Castle Garden. After this it served as an immigrant depot, preceding Ellis Island. Then it was remodeled by McKim, Mead & White to serve as an aquarium. It now has been restored as a fort, exhibiting this handsome doorway influenced by French military architecture of the sixteenth century.

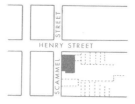

SAINT AUGUSTINE'S CHAPEL (formerly All Saints Church) Southeast corner Henry and Scammel streets. This small church shows its architectural kinship to the nearby Sea and Land Church in that both, though basically Georgian, boast Gothic windows, a sophistication derived from English precedent, perhaps from the plates of Battey Langley's books. Small stones were used here as at Saint Paul's Chapel, and, although ashlar quoins were omitted, the window openings have been reinforced with brick frames. The spire was apparently not completed above the stonework, as the wooden spire would seem to date from a much later period.

SAINT LUKE'S CHAPEL   483 Hudson Street. Notable as a fine early instance of town planning, this chapel was built with its flanking houses to form an attractive group of buildings. Although its extreme simplicity denotes no particular style of architecture, it is best described as a simplified or vernacular version of the Federal style.

WEST BUILDING, GENERAL THEOLOGICAL SEMINARY Ninth Avenue and West 20th Street. This building was one of an identical pair, the East Building having been razed many years ago. It is one of the earliest Gothic Revival buildings in the city and displays a rather naïve application of Gothic ornament. Although it is an early forerunner of the countless ivy-clad campuses of the nineteen-twenties, it is, through its simplicity, closer to many of them than were the later, more elaborate Gothic buildings of the eighteen-sixties.

SAINT JAMES' CHURCH   Saint James Street near Chatham Square. One of the finest of the Greek Revival churches in Manhattan, it has been attributed to Minard Lafever because of the beauty of its detail. The porch is recessed between wide flanking sidewalls, as is the case with Saint John's in the Village (see page 98), only this church is simple distyle in antis of the Doric order.

INDIA HOUSE   Hanover Square. This magnificent building was one of the first to be erected on Hanover Square after the disastrous fire of 1835. It was probably built by Richard F. Carman, who was listed in city directories as a carpenter and who reputedly amassed a fortune rebuilding the "burnt district" in 1836. He later had a country seat at Fort Washington and developed Carmanville. India House seems to have been built as an office block, being occupied subsequently by the Hanover Bank and the New York Cotton Exchange. Today it is a private club which houses a superb maritime museum.

SAINT PETER'S (Roman Catholic) **CHURCH**   Southeast corner Barclay and Church streets.
A full-fledged example of the Greek Revival in temple form executed in stone. The great
dignity of this church is at once apparent. The shafts of the columns consist of only three
drums, each one about ten feet tall. Such large pieces of stone usually came in by barge and
were brought up from the river on horse-drawn drays.

SAINT JOHN'S IN THE VILLAGE Southwest corner Waverly Place and West 11th Street. The Greek Revival made several modifications in the conventional Greek temple form. Where the width of a building might have required six columns (hexastyle) and the cost of erecting them was prohibitive, the scheme of bringing the sidewalls forward (in antis) and using two columns (distyle) was followed; the balance of the width was met by widening as much as required on each side of the portico, with flush walls parallel to the street. These walls were the unusual feature, resulting in an exceedingly handsome innovation. This church is distyle in antis, combined with prostyle tetrastyle (having four columns).

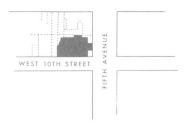

WEST 10TH STREET

FIFTH AVENUE

CHURCH OF THE ASCENSION   Northwest corner Fifth Avenue and West 10th Street. Particularly beautiful for its interior and for the great mural by John La Farge above the altar, this church is a good example of the Gothic Revival style in ecclesiastical architecture. It appears that the rector, knowing architect Richard Upjohn's High Church proclivities, bought the lot across the end of the property for his rectory in order to prevent Upjohn from building a deep chancel, as was his wont.

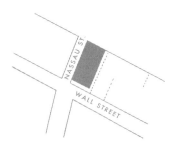

FEDERAL HALL NATIONAL MEMORIAL (formerly United States Subtreasury Building) Northeast corner Wall and Nassau streets. To place a circular rotunda in a rectangular building may seem illogical, but such were the vagaries of the Greek Revival. It was originally planned to build a Roman dome over the rotunda, set squarely in the middle of this Greek temple. The dome was never built, but the handsome rotunda may still be seen. This building is located on the site of the old Federal Hall, a Federal Style building designed by Major L'Enfant, on whose balcony George Washington took the oath of office as President.

GRACE CHURCH Northeast corner Broadway and East 10th Street. One of the few buildings in New York that closes a vista, this church has a spire that may be seen from far down lower Broadway. Architecturally, it is one of the monuments of the Gothic Revival, complete with rectory and parish house. Although private pews were recently abolished, it was once the most popular church with New York society, and its pews, reigned over by the famous Sexton Brown, sold at a premium.

VILLAGE PRESBYTERIAN CHURCH   143 West 13th Street. The simulation of stone in wood required that the carpenters produce absolutely flat, smooth surfaces for parts of the entablature and for the back of the pediment. Where these surfaces were not properly maintained and kept painted, the whole illusion was lost. In this hexastyle Doric church it was apparently not deemed necessary to return the entablature beyond the depth of the portico, as this was not a corner site.

CHURCH OF THE HOLY COMMUNION Northeast corner Sixth Avenue and West 20th Street. Rarely does such a complete ecclesiastical group survive intact from the Gothic Revival. Although this diminutive church, parish house, and rectory represent that style pared down to its bare essentials, the general effect is delightful and sincerely religious in its lack of pretentiousness.

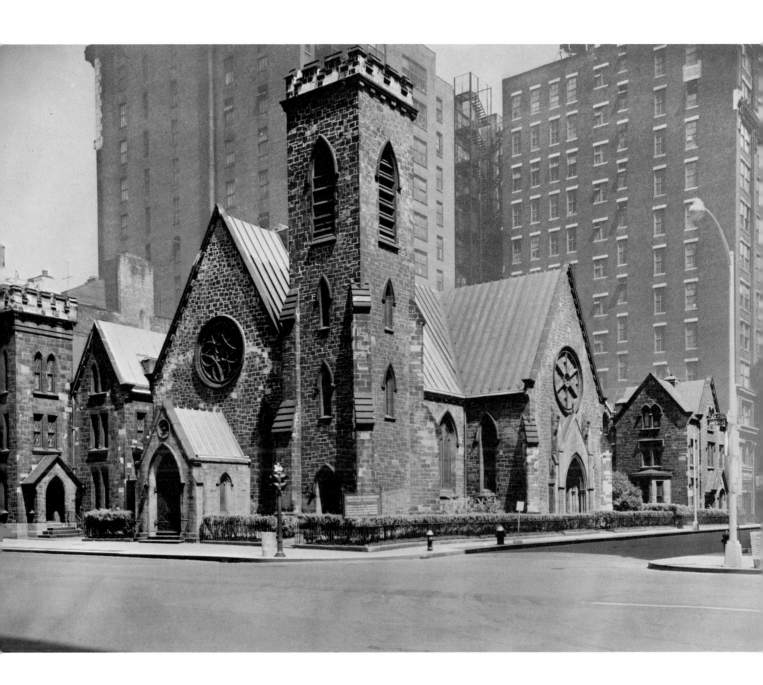

CHURCH OF THE HOLY APOSTLES   Southeast corner Ninth Avenue and West 28th Street. Extremely deceptive with regard to its age, this church looks as though it might have been built even as late as 1910. Actually, it was erected in the eighteen-forties in a very free, dynamic style using an ingenious array of bull's-eyes, curved pediments, and corbels. An indication that Minard Lafever may have been its architect is found in Plate XCVIII of his book *The Architectural Instructor,* published in 1856, where we see a small rural church that is quite similar in character.

TRINITY CHURCH Broadway at Wall Street. The present is the third Episcopal church on this site. Its spire was long a landmark on the horizon. Today we see it surrounded by high buildings, which tend to dwarf it, although in its day it was quite a large church. The quality of the Gothic Revival is well exemplified by the rather naïve detail, the plaster vaults, and the traceried windows. The beautiful bronze doors, added at a later date under the supervision of Richard Morris Hunt, depict biblical scenes based on Italian precedent. That all the figures on the doors are not biblical is testified to by a little head on the frame of the right-hand door; here we find the sculptor Karl Bitter's "cher patron," Hunt himself, with his pointed beard.

WEST 12TH STREET

FIFTH AVENUE

WEST 11TH STREET

FIRST PRESBYTERIAN CHURCH Fifth Avenue between West 11th and West 12th streets. Set in ample grounds where it may be seen from three sides, this handsome exemplar of the Gothic Revival makes us realize that all was not necessarily fuss and gingerbread in this period. Joseph C. Wells, the architect, attempted a scholarly representation of an ecclesiastical style which, at best, was foreign to this country before 1835.

CAST-IRON BUILDING (Edgar Laing Stores) Northwest corner Washington and Murray streets. The great architectural significance of this small group of warehouses is too little known. It was built in 1848 by James Bogardus on a patented system he had devised. Here we see the first complete, self-supporting cast-iron façades erected in New York. This building has a timber floor and does not incorporate Bogardus' patented iron floor system, which he later used in conjunction with iron façades for his Eccentric Mill on Centre Street; nonetheless, it was a pioneer structure.

OLD ASTOR LIBRARY 425 Lafayette Street. Before it was combined with the Tilden Trust and the Lenox Library to form the nucleus of the New York Public Library in 1912, the Astor Library had been at this location since the eighteen-fifties. The central portion of this handsome Italianate structure was built by John Jacob Astor; his sons added the north and south wings at a later period. It now houses the Hebrew Sheltering and Immigrant Aid Society.

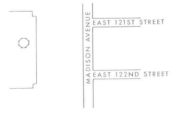

WATCHTOWER Mount Morris Park. Using the same post-and-lintel type of construction that he had employed for his cast-iron warehouses (see page 116), James Bogardus designed many iron fire towers like this, to replace the older ones of wood. They were once distributed throughout the city, and the tower on the Jefferson Market Courthouse was also intended as a fire lookout. This tower was set in its present location at the time the terraces in Mount Morris Park were constructed.

WEST 29TH STREET FIFTH AVENUE

MARBLE COLLEGIATE CHURCH Northwest corner Fifth Avenue and West 29th Street. Designated by its architect, Samuel A. Warner, as a Romanesque church, this is an early example of the first phase of the Romanesque Revival — a style which, in the hands of Henry Hobson Richardson, was destined to become powerful and original in expression.

TRINITY CHAPEL (Serbian [Eastern Orthodox] Cathedral of Saint Sava) 21 West 25th Street. Designed by Richard Upjohn, the architect of Trinity Church on Broadway, this chapel is one of the finer evocations of the Gothic Revival. The straightforward design utilizes wood trusses instead of simulated rib vaulting. The handsome yet simple apse provides a fine setting for the altar and closes the long nave of the chapel most effectively.

E. V. HAUGHWOUT & CO. BUILDING Northeast corner Broadway and Broome Street. In 1857 the first practicable passenger elevator to be installed in a mercantile establishment was put in operation in this building. Haughwout's boasted a fine line of glass, china, and silverware. Its proud exterior, harbinger of the endless vista, is somewhat reminiscent of Sansovino's Library on the Piazetta in Venice. The attempt to borrow beauty from the Continent, for even such newfangled structures as these cast-iron buildings, was indicative of our lack of assurance in the direction of our own architectural development.

COOPER UNION Cooper Square and Astor Place. This building was specially designed to house Peter Cooper's great philanthropy — a trade school for boys in New York who could not otherwise afford such specialized training. It is notable for the early use of rolled-iron sections produced by Cooper, Hewitt & Co. at Trenton, New Jersey — Cooper's own rolling mills. Cooper put off the completion of the school to roll beams for Astor's new library on Lafayette Street and for Harper & Brothers' publishing house on Franklin Square.

IRON BRIDGE Central Park. There is a storybook quality about the iron bridges in Central Park, and a gaiety which suggests ladies with parasols and children with hoops passing over them. This one, Gothic in inspiration, is a remarkably free piece of design and shows the versatility of cast iron when used in free-flowing forms.

CHURCH OF THE INCARNATION   Northeast corner Madison Avenue and East 35th Street. Rather late for Gothic Revival, this church nonetheless owes its inspiration to that period. The introduction of incised ornament foreshadows Neo-Grec design, which was to become so fashionable in the 'seventies.

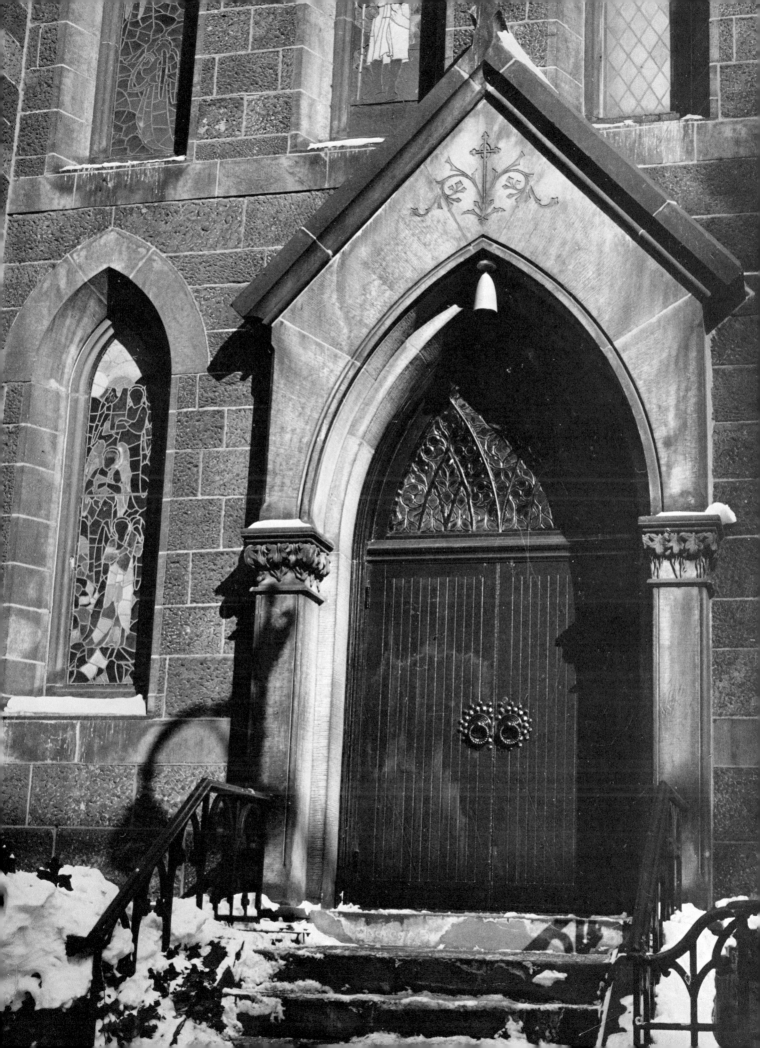

MANHATTAN CLUB Southeast corner Madison Avenue and East 26th Street. This house, which attempted to re-create the glories of Second Empire Paris, was built by Leonard W. Jerome as the American Jockey Club, complete with stables and a small private theatre. It later became the University Club and is now the home of the Manhattan Club. Jerome's grandson, child of his daughter Jennie and her husband Lord Randolph Churchill, became the greatest of all Britain's Prime Ministers.

NATIONAL ARTS CLUB 15 Gramercy Park. Designed by Vaux and Radford for Samuel J. Tilden, the two town houses now combined at this address were executed in a scholarly version of Ruskinian Gothic. They display on the exteriors a carefully modulated banding of polychromy replete with foliated sculpture and medallions containing busts of famous authors. The interiors are very rich and to our tastes gloomy, abounding in highly original foliate carvings. There is an exquisite glass dome in the westerly house.

JEFFERSON MARKET COURTHOUSE Southwest corner Sixth Avenue and West 10th Street. The courthouse and watchtower which we see today is all that remains of a complex of buildings which once included, in addition, a market and a jail. These buildings, on their triangular site, were all designed in a uniform style and represented a remarkably coherent piece of town planning carried out by the city government. The style can best be described as Victorian Gothic.

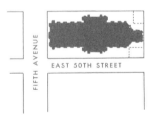

FIFTH AVENUE

EAST 50TH STREET

SAINT PATRICK'S CATHEDRAL   Fifth Avenue between East 50th and East 51st streets. James Renwick Jr., son of Professor Renwick of Columbia College and himself an architect, was probably one of the best-equipped architects in New York to undertake the stupendous task of designing a stone cathedral in Manhattan. The construction alone extended over a period of some twenty years, and the result was a fairly competent copy of a French Gothic cathedral, adapted to American needs.

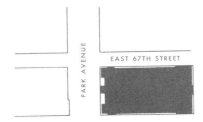

SEVENTH REGIMENT ARMORY Park and Lexington avenues between East 66th and East 67th streets. This indefensible fort, bristling with battlements, provides an amusing commentary on the architectural expressionism of the 'seventies, although a functional drill hall makes up for its defensive shortcomings. A high belfry above the central tower has been removed and the tower has been lowered since the turn of the century.

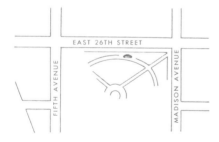

FARRAGUT MONUMENT Madison Square. This monument represents the collaboration of the sculptor Augustus Saint-Gaudens and the architect Stanford White, who designed the base. We readily sense the stance of a seafarer braced on deck to withstand the rolling sea. The base, with its beautiful lettering, sea-drenched maidens, and dolphins, is a superb allegory unique in its style at that date and foreshadowing the Continental Art Nouveau.

WEST 23RD STREET

SEVENTH AVENUE

CHELSEA HOTEL 222 West 23rd Street. Designed as an apartment house by the once noted firm of Hubert, Pirsson & Co., which also designed the great "Spanish Flats" at Central Park South and Seventh Avenue, this is probably the only building that in any way resembles that structure although its iron balconies are unique. In style it is best described as Victorian Gothic, but in some of its details it shows elements of the Queen Anne or Free Classic style that was destined to become so fashionable in the 'eighties.

BROOKLYN BRIDGE City Hall Square, Manhattan, to Parkes Cadman Plaza, Brooklyn. Usually described as Gothic Revival in style, the towers of the bridge, seemingly battered with crowning mouldings, are also somewhat reminiscent of Egyptian pylons. Montgomery Schuyler, well-known architectural critic of the turn of the century, criticized the towers for widening at the top, just where the iron saddles demanded an insweeping profile to follow the line of the cables; yet Roebling's design is visually very effective and powerful.

VILLARD MANSION   Madison Avenue between East 50th and East 51st streets. This great complex of town houses surrounding a central courtyard was designed by Joseph M. Wells for McKim, Mead & White in the manner of an early sixteenth-century Italian palazzo. By far the most beautiful feature of this block of residences is the interior decoration of Henry Villard's own house on the south side of the courtyard.

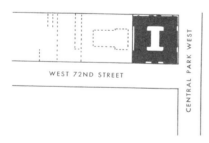

DAKOTA APARTMENTS Central Park West between West 72nd and West 73rd streets. The first of the great super-block apartments with central drive-in courtyard, this building was virtually without precedent. It was designed in the early eighteen-eighties by Henry Janeway Hardenbergh in the high manner of the nineteenth-century German Renaissance. He later designed the Plaza Hotel (see page 228).

DeVINNE PRESS BUILDING Northeast corner Lafayette and East 4th streets. Home of the famous DeVinne Press, which produced such handsome books in its day, this Romanesque Revival structure, with its low gable end emphasized by the little arches rising beneath it, set a vogue for commercial and industrial buildings that proved a fine, expressive solution for the low-pitched roof. The Judge Building on Fifth Avenue followed suit, as did many others of less note.

ISAAC VAIL BROKAW RESIDENCE   Northeast corner Fifth Avenue and East 79th Street. This little castle on its corner site is one of the few remaining town houses which could boast such splendid isolation. Romanesque in many of its details, this mansion is basically of French Renaissance inspiration in its fenestration and roof lines. The marble interiors clove to the Romanesque Revival and were some of the finest and most original work of this style.

SAINT GEORGE'S PARISH HOUSE 207 East 16th Street. The picturesque massing of this building ingeniously enfolds the diverse functions of the parish house. With his expressive use of masonry, Leopold Eidlitz has given us another fine building to complement the dignity of the great church.

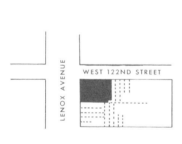

SAINT MARTIN'S CHURCH   Southeast corner Lenox Avenue and West 122nd Street. Probably the best Romanesque Revival church in Manhattan since Saint Agnes' Chapel was razed, this Harlem church boasts the second-finest carillon in the city. Unfortunately, a fire destroyed the beautiful original interiors.

AMERICAN MUSEUM OF NATURAL HISTORY, SOUTH ENTRANCE West 77th Street between Central Park West and Columbus Avenue. The Romanesque Revival was well suited to large, imposing effects; and here, with its flanking engaged towers and huge segmental arch, the entrance is handsomely featured.

WEST 43RD STREET   FIFTH AVENUE

CENTURY ASSOCIATION   7 West 43rd Street. Despite its rather fussy detail, the main massing of this façade, with its once deeply recessed Palladian arched loggia, is extremely masterful and teaches a lesson in the successful combination of elements. McKim, Mead & White designed this building when the Club moved from East 15th Street; they achieved great elegance in its sumptuous interiors.

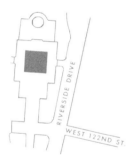

GENERAL GRANT NATIONAL MEMORIAL　Riverside Drive at West 122nd Street. The upper part of this imposing tomb, designed in competition, is reminiscent of that of King Mausolos at Halicarnassos, although the basic proportions and shape have been somewhat modified. The interior recalls Napoleon's tomb in the chapel of the Invalides in Paris, carried out on a much smaller scale.

WASHINGTON SQUARE SOUTH

THOMPSON STREET

JUDSON MEMORIAL CHURCH   Southwest corner Washington Square South and Thompson Street. When McKim, Mead & White brought a note of gaiety to a drab city of brownstones with Madison Square Garden, they introduced the best of the Italian Renaissance to New York. It was followed by an ever increasing series of handsome buildings and churches, of which this group with its campanile is one of the finest.

THE PLAYERS (CLUB) 16 Gramercy Park South. Originally a Gothic Revival town house, this building was purchased by Edwin Booth for his home. In 1888 he made it into a clubhouse for his actor friends. At about this time Stanford White offered his services in remodeling the interior and adding the Italian Renaissance loggia and lanterns, which provide such a handsome entrance.

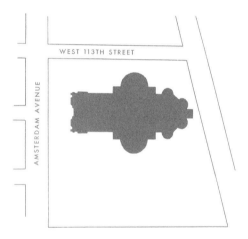

CATHEDRAL CHURCH OF SAINT JOHN THE DIVINE   Cathedral Heights. In competition among most of the leading architects of the day, the magnificent Romanesque Revival scheme of Heins and La Farge was selected for construction of an American cathedral. Only the choir and apse and a rough masonry shell at the crossing were completed when Ralph Adams Cram gained control of the design for the rest of the building, which is now being carried out in French Gothic style. The map shown here is that of the original prize-winning Romanesque design.

CHURCH MISSIONS' HOUSE Southeast corner Fourth Avenue and East 22nd Street. If we were to seek the precedent for the hordes of commercial Gothic structures which invaded Manhattan in the early 'twenties, we might well find it in this handsome building, soon to be abandoned by the New York (Protestant Episcopal) Mission Society. Its clearly articulated expression of structure and its uninhibited verticality gave new promise for the future of American architecture.

FIFTH AVENUE

EAST 60TH STREET

METROPOLITAN CLUB Northeast corner Fifth Avenue and East 60th Street. Reputedly founded by J. P. Morgan for the benefit of a friend who had been denied membership in another club, this palazzo has long been known as the "Millionaires' Club." The exterior with its gates and carriage turn-around is extremely handsome and expressive. The interior, despite its sumptuousness, has certain failings in proportion though not in its details. The marble-lined great hall, which is relatively narrow, extends up several stories, producing a sensation of excessive height.

WASHINGTON ARCH Fifth Avenue at Washington Square. Originally erected in staff and plaster by Stanford White in celebration of the hundredth anniversary of Washington's inauguration as President, the arch found such popular favor that it was rebuilt in permanent materials. Statues of Washington in war and peace face northward up the Avenue, and it is interesting to note the freedom in the design of the panels behind them relative to the otherwise Classical design.

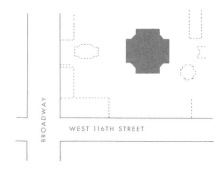

LOW LIBRARY Columbia University, West 116th Street between Broadway and Amsterdam Avenue. When he first saw this building, Louis Sullivan said, "Surely this is the waxworks of architecture." Yet, as the center of the campus, the Low Library, modeled after the Pantheon at Rome, is extremely successful in unifying the entire scheme. With the advent of the new library, Butler Hall, it has become an administration center. Its handsome central rotunda creates a fine setting for various University activities.

CHURCH OF THE HOLY TRINITY (Rhinelander Memorial) 312 East 88th Street. This remarkable group of buildings, carried out by the firm of Barney & Chapman as a uniform scheme, forms an extremely effective whole despite the rather fussy treatment of French Gothic and the fact that the parish buildings are French Renaissance in inspiration. The bell tower, with its uninterrupted verticality, is one of the finest in the city.

UNIVERSITY CLUB   Northwest corner Fifth Avenue and West 54th Street. Of all the buildings in New York which have been influenced by the Italian Renaissance, this club probably comes closest to resembling a sixteenth-century palazzo; yet despite this fact, the combination of details is quite original.

NEW YORK YACHT CLUB 37 West 44th Street. A fanciful version of Beaux Arts architecture, the main façade introduces, between columns, a series of bay windows in the form of sixteenth-century galleon sterns. The pergola which once graced the third floor contributed a further air of lightness and gaiety to this club designed by Warren & Wetmore.

BAYARD (CONDICT) BUILDING 65–69 Bleecker Street. The only New York building designed by Louis Sullivan, it represents an executed portion of a much larger building he had once planned for a trust and savings bank in the Midwest. The terra-cotta cornice, with its supporting angels, was an extremely interesting solution of the problem of how to handle the top of a building — a question which was of great concern to the architects of the 'eighties and 'nineties.

LOTOS CLUB 5 East 66th Street. Built as a private residence, this house shows the most ornate phase of the Beaux Arts style as expressed by many of our architects. The desire to make an elaborate display of details, modified for the sake of originality, often led us up a blind alley.

APPELLATE DIVISION OF THE SUPREME COURT OF NEW YORK Northeast corner Madison Avenue and East 25th Street. Extremely rich in its use of materials, this small courthouse seems almost overburdened by its pediment and balustrade crowned with statues. Yet it is significant as a building in which the arts, including sculpture and mural painting, were liberally represented through the efforts of the Municipal Art Society.

METROPOLITAN MUSEUM OF ART, CENTRAL PORTION   Fifth Avenue opposite East 82nd
Street. The enormous scale of this façade is reminiscent of the main hall of a Roman public
bath and forms a dramatic setting for the entrance to this great museum. The huge blocks
of stone above the columns were intended for sculpture which was never executed. Richard
Morris Hunt, dean of New York architects, designed it and once remarked that he would
wish to have it considered his monument.

SOLDIERS AND SAILORS MONUMENT Riverside Drive at West 89th Street. Typical reminder, in its hollow pomposity, of an army which had not been engaged in a major struggle since 1865 and of the exploits of the Great White Fleet, this monument symbolized the stolid wealth and prosperity of our country at the time of its building.

EAST 51ST STREET

PARK AVENUE

SAINT BARTHOLOMEW'S CHURCH Park Avenue between East 50th and East 51st streets. When the new Saint Bartholomew's was built in the nineteen-twenties, the handsome entrances, designed in 1902 for the earlier church, were moved from Madison Avenue and incorporated in the new structure. They were inspired by the Romanesque Church of Saint Giles at Arles, France, and blended singularly well with the Byzantine splendor of the new edifice. The tower of the General Electric Building, which rises directly behind Saint Bartholomew's, used the same warm-colored brick as the church to harmonize with it — a farsighted bit of planning rarely encountered today.

FLATIRON (FULLER) BUILDING Junction of Broadway and Fifth Avenue at East 23rd Street. Located on a site once known as "the Cow Catcher," this building amazed New Yorkers with its dizzy, slender height as seen from the north. Actually, it was almost as sturdy as a rectangular building, though triangular in plan. The exterior treatment, overly rich to our modern eyes, was considered quite conservative in 1902 when it was designed by D. H. Burnham & Company.

MRS. ORME WILSON RESIDENCE   3 East 64th Street. This fine town house clearly expresses on the exterior the functions within, ranging from the grand drawing room windows on the second floor to the tiny oval dormers of the attic.

WEST 74TH STREET

BROADWAY

ANSONIA APARTMENTS Broadway between West 73rd and West 74th streets. Strolling along
upper Broadway, we are startled at this evocation of Paris with its gay towers and great
mansard roofs. Yet there is one great difference: where such a building in Paris might not
stand more than six or seven stories high, here, in its American version, it towers to a
height of seventeen stories. Designed by the firm of Graves & Duboy for W. E. D. Stokes,
it is a happy contribution to our street architecture.

ST. REGIS HOTEL Southeast corner Fifth Avenue and East 55th Street. If one had sought out the most handsomely decorated hotel in Manhattan in the early nineteen-hundreds, one might well have turned to the new St. Regis, where rich marbles, bronze, and wood were displayed in a series of splendid salons, corridors, and suites designed by the firm of Trowbridge & Livingston. Today these glowing bronze doors still greet the visitor on arrival.

NEW YORK STOCK EXCHANGE   Broad and Wall streets. Contained in this building we find, paradoxically, a complete sculptured pediment of Classic inspiration and what was probably the first all-glass curtain wall in New York. The pediment figures were executed by the sculptor J. Q. A. Ward, assisted by Paul W. Bartlett. The glass curtain wall, placed directly behind the colonnade, provides light for the great floor of the Exchange itself.

SEVENTY-FIRST REGIMENT ARMORY   Southeast corner Park Avenue and East 34th Street. The Armory, although basically Romanesque in design, flaunts a very high Mediaeval Italian tower complete with machicolations and American flags built into the masonry at the top as a decorative element. The architect reputedly asked his little son what he thought ought to go at the top of the tower, to which he replied, "Flags, Daddy" — and there they are, permanently affixed for all to behold.

NEW YORK TIMES BUILDING West 42nd Street between Broadway and Seventh Avenue. Designed by Cyrus L. W. Eidlitz, son of the noted architect Leopold Eidlitz, this building overcame several structural difficulties in the construction of its foundations. In style it is reminiscent of the Italian Renaissance, with corbeled cornice and decorative detail. On a similar site, it repeated the theme of the Flatiron Building (see page 200), although with less visual daring.

MORGAN LIBRARY 29 East 36th Street. Built expressly to house the famous J. Pierpont Morgan Collection of books and manuscripts, the Morgan Library was designed by McKim, Mead & White to provide a beautiful setting for the treasures within. As in the construction of Greek temples, the stones were perfectly fitted, obviating the use of a full bed of mortar — an expensive but enduring method of constructing masonry walls and today practically a lost art.

WEST 44TH STREET

FIFTH AVENUE

HARVARD CLUB 27 West 44th Street. Originally designed by McKim as a discreet Georgian building of modest scale, it stands on a block where it once enjoyed as neighbors the Racquet Club, the Academy of Medicine, and the Berkeley School. Two wings were added behind it at a later date. Harvard Hall is probably one of the largest rooms in any club in New York, extending three stories in height, and in length the depth of a normal townhouse lot. The Florentine quality of the design, the two great fireplaces, and the tapestries all lend an air of subdued richness and warmth to this fine room.

LADY CHAPEL, SAINT PATRICK'S CATHEDRAL Madison Avenue between East 50th and East 51st streets. A sophisticated version of French Gothic architecture, this delicate little chapel attaches itself as a jewel to the coarser fabric of the cathedral proper. It reminds us of that period of mediaeval architecture when the builders were straining stone masonry construction to the limit in order to achieve new effects of lightness and daring.

EVENING POST BUILDING   20 Vesey Street. The Art Nouveau found little favor in New York, yet it offered many new possibilities to the designer. Here a beautiful expression of the under-lying structure was combined with a novel, free-flowing design which subtly emphasized the vertical by means of elongation, both in the sculptured figures and in the niches behind them.

GORHAM BUILDING   Southwest corner Fifth Avenue and West 36th Street. One of the outstanding masterpieces of New York architecture, this Italian Renaissance building by Mc-Kim, Mead & White ingeniously adapts the first-floor arcade to show windows. The magnificent sense of scale which is established above by the windows, screens, balconies, and cornice leaves one with a sense of accomplished finality all too rarely achieved. This photograph was taken before the building was altered, but the changes cannot completely destroy the dignity of this old aristocrat.

METROPOLITAN LIFE INSURANCE COMPANY TOWER   Madison Square. New York boasts few campaniles, yet here the architects arrived at the ingenious scheme of combining sky-scraper offices, a commercial symbol ("The Light that Never Fails"), and a large office building into one structure. In 1908 it was the tallest building in New York, and the clock faces are larger than those of Big Ben in London. This photo shows the tower before it was remodeled.

APTHORPE APARTMENTS Broadway and West End Avenue between West 78th and West 79th streets. Following the lead of the Dakota on Central Park West (see page 152), many new apartment houses were built with large central courtyards. This one, which occupies an entire city block, was remodeled several years ago, splitting each apartment into two. The division of rooms was balanced by using the living room and bedrooms for one new apartment and the dining room, kitchen, and maids' rooms for the other. This ingenious scheme produced two fully remodeled apartments where only one existed formerly.

NEW YORK PUBLIC LIBRARY Fifth Avenue between West 40th and West 42nd streets. This building probably comes nearer than any other in America to the complete realization of Beaux Arts design at its best. Replete with sparkle and delicacy, with its urns, fountains, sculpture, and ornament, it is by night or day a joyous creation. Unlike the legion of heavy Classical buildings that invaded the country after the World's Columbian Exposition, it has somehow managed to keep the light, airy quality which so often is seen only in architectural drawings, so rarely achieved in execution.

FIRST NATIONAL CITY BANK 55 Wall Street. When the great fire of 1835 ravaged a large part of lower Manhattan, Town and Davis' beautiful Merchants' Exchange on Wall Street was completely gutted. The merchants resolved to rebuild it on a grander scale in fireproof construction. The great Ionic colonnade above the granite base is original. After several years it was occupied by the United States Government Customs House. It was remodeled as we see it today, with its upper floors added, by McKim, Mead & White for the National City Bank.

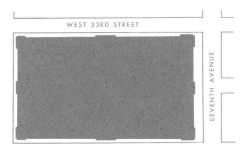

WEST 33RD STREET

SEVENTH AVENUE

PENNSYLVANIA STATION (OUTER CONCOURSE) Seventh and Eighth avenues between West 31st and West 33rd streets. This great concourse of steel and glass is one of the few reminders we have of a once practical and expressive design for railroad architecture. The precedent for such an enclosure is found in the train sheds which were located over the tracks in many of the older terminals. Here, in this great station, it was particularly well suited to its use as a pedestrian concourse, giving a wonderful sense of openness and light. It may soon be demolished to make way for a remodeled station.

BLACK, STARR & FROST BUILDING Southwest corner Fifth Avenue and West 48th Street. Designed expressly as a showcase for jewelry, this building has always provided an exquisite background for the display of gems and silverware. The simple show windows are well set off between handsome piers which lead the eye up to one of the most beautiful cornices in Manhattan.

VANDERBILT HOTEL Park Avenue between East 33rd and East 34th streets. Once the New York home of Enrico Caruso and other notables, this hotel, in its use of brick and terra cotta, evokes memories of the best of the new architecture of the early 'twenties which it inspired. The Adamesque detail of the windows and lanterns suggests an English precedent, while the glass sunburst marquee that once graced the entrance represented the epitome of elegance.

MRS. JAMES B. DUKE RESIDENCE Northeast corner Fifth Avenue and East 78th Street. When Horace Trumbauer, the Philadelphia architect, was asked to design a town house for the Duke family, his firm chose as the model a house in Bordeaux, modifying its proportions to suit the site. Some of the handsomest buildings ever erected in New York were designed by his firm. They included Eleanor Widener's house, now razed, at 901 Fifth Avenue; the Herbert N. Straus house at 9 East 71st Street; the Wildenstein Galleries at 19 East 64th Street; and the old Duveen Galleries, which once stood at the northwest corner of Fifth Avenue and West 56th Street. Many of his designs were directly inspired by those of the French architect Jacques Ange Gabriel.

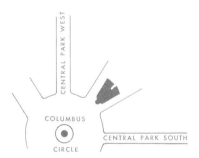

MAINE MEMORIAL   Columbus Circle at West 59th Street. This unusual memorial, designed by H. Van Buren Magonigle, boasts some of the finest sculpture in the city; it was executed by Attilio Piccirilli. There is a brooding quality of sorrow in some of the adult figures completely belied by the vigorous youth arising, a symbol of hope, at the prow.

GUARANTY TRUST BUILDING 140 Broadway. Here the colossal Ionic order, set off by simple ashlar masonry walls, lends great dignity to the front façade, while an equally handsome colonnade screens the windows of the main banking room along Liberty Street. York & Sawyer proved their versatility in departing from their Romanesque mode for this more purely Classical theme.

PARK PLACE

BROADWAY

WOOLWORTH BUILDING 233 Broadway. Of all the architectural styles, the Gothic seemed to lend itself best to skyscraper design. Cass Gilbert, using his West Street Building (Brady Building) as a trial balloon, arrived at a remarkably expressive result in this high, self-washing, terra-cotta-clad building.

GRAND CENTRAL TERMINAL East 42nd Street between Vanderbilt and Lexington avenues. Here is a case in which distinguished architecture and a brilliant engineering solution were wedded to produce one of the fabulous railroad terminals of our times. Grand Central was always a place one was proud to show to out-of-town visitors until the mean clutter of shops and displays ruined its once magnificent interior scale. Nonetheless, the exterior windows, with their great expanses of glass and steel, represent the best of Parisian Beaux Arts architecture.

SAINT THOMAS' CHURCH Northwest corner Fifth Avenue and West 53rd Street. Despite its asymmetrical composition, with only one tower, this church is such a beautiful example of French Gothic architecture that we are hardly aware of the lack of a second tower. The plan is ingeniously arranged and has functioned successfully for the congregation and for some of the most fashionable weddings in New York.

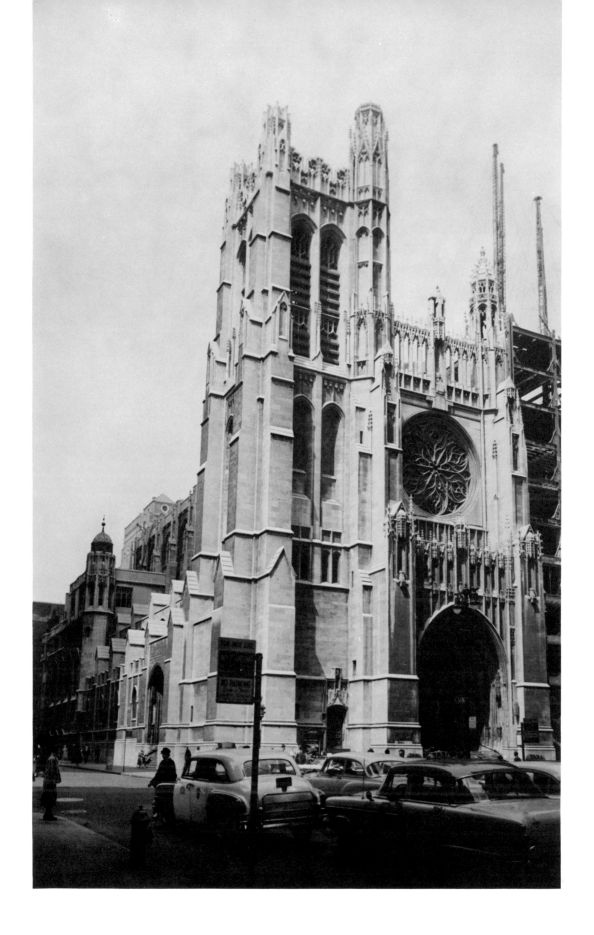

WILLIAM STARR MILLER RESIDENCE   Southeast corner Fifth Avenue and East 86th Street. One of the most attractive phases of French Classic architecture was that of the period of Louis XIII, which we see in the Place des Vosges in Paris. This style retained a quality of domestic warmth which disappeared with the frigid elegance of the all-limestone creations of later periods.

FIFTH AVENUE

EAST 94TH STREET

WILLARD STRAIGHT RESIDENCE Northeast corner Fifth Avenue and East 94th Street. This large, sunny dwelling is an excellent example of the American town house at its best. The bull's-eye windows at the top lend an air of novelty to an otherwise conservative Federal design. The interior woodwork is extremely fine and demonstrates the loving care with which Delano and Aldrich executed their commissions.

KNICKERBOCKER CLUB Southeast corner Fifth Avenue and East 62nd Street. Typical of the fine sensitivity in the work of Delano and Aldrich is this handsome re-creation of a Federal town house. The beautiful brickwork is excellently set off by the marble lintels and iron balconies at the windows.

EAST 52ND STREET

PARK AVENUE

RACQUET AND TENNIS CLUB Park Avenue between East 52nd and East 53rd streets. This very fine adaptation of a Florentine palazzo was the work of McKim, Mead & White. Although it contains all the indoor facilities of a modern American athletic club, it is a handsome addition to the broad thoroughfare of Park Avenue. Despite the fact that it is low, it is completely in scale with its contemporaries and with the giants that today surround it.

FIFTH AVENUE

EAST 91ST STREET

OTTO KAHN RESIDENCE Northeast corner Fifth Avenue and East 91st Street. One of the largest private houses ever built in Manhattan, this Italian palazzo, including a drive-in for automobiles, has a modest self-effacing quality, due to the uniformity of its architectural effect, which makes it possible to pass and repass it many times without realizing what it is. In this respect it represents the epitome of restrained good taste.

EAST 42ND STREET

LEXINGTON AVENUE

BOWERY SAVINGS BANK 110 East 42nd Street. The architectural firm of York & Sawyer made a name for itself designing a series of Romanesque buildings easily recognized on the exterior by their superb rustication, and by their rich, colorful interiors. Here, in the main banking room, we see a variegated assortment of marble columns. Historically it will be remembered that the Romanesque architects looted the temples of classical antiquity of their rich marbles and polished columns to produce their new buildings.

AMERICAN RADIATOR BUILDING   40 West 40th Street. One of the greatest problems that confronted our architects was how best to express skyscraper construction. Here there was no precedent, so that many interesting experiments were made, among which this was one of the most notable. Raymond Hood, using a theme of black and gold, achieved the "new look" for the 'twenties; and, although the setbacks above seem to us needlessly agitated, the general effect was original and fairly expressive of the underlying structure. The small, sculptured corbels just above street level are interesting as ornament although by no means original.

WEST 77TH STREET   CENTRAL PARK WEST

ROOSEVELT MEMORIAL, AMERICAN MUSEUM OF NATURAL HISTORY   Central Park West between West 77th and West 81st streets. The huge triumphal-arch motif is the work of John Russell Pope, designer par excellence of classical monuments. The sweeping wing-walls in front of the building with their charming bas-reliefs, and the powerful equestrian statue of "T. R." by James Earle Fraser, lend great dignity to the ensemble, making one immediately aware of the colossal scale of the main entrance.

DAILY NEWS BUILDING   220 East 42nd Street. Acclaimed for its verticality, this building was considered by many as the embodiment of the soaring quality of the skyscraper. However, the vertical ribbons of equal width fail to express the location of the steel columns; and, as seen from within, the fenestration — a series of solids and voids — represents no improvement over that of the eighteenth century.

NEW YORK COUNTY LAWYERS ASSOCIATION   14 Vesey Street. This very handsome little
building, although basically an eclectic version of Federal architecture, is executed in stone
instead of brick and vaunts a fine row of Corinthian pilasters, floral swags, and medallions.
These features are reminiscent of Adamesque design and British prototypes.

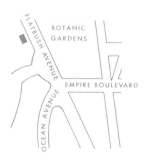

LEFFERTS HOMESTEAD Prospect Park near Flatbush Avenue. Although this is basically a Dutch Colonial farmhouse, we are amazed at the beauty of the detail of the main entrance, where delicate colonnettes and exquisite reeding set off leaded lights and a fine Dutch door.

NO ADM
TO CH
UNDER 14
WITHOU
FOODSTUFF
IN BU

FLATBUSH DUTCH REFORMED CHURCH Southwest corner Flatbush and Church avenues. As in Saint Paul's Chapel, Manhattan, the most noteworthy architectural features of this church are the spire and the interior. Surrounded by its little cemetery, it creates a picture of the church, unchanged since it was built, perfect in its original setting.

HOSPITAL, NEW YORK NAVY YARD 263 Flushing Avenue. A free interpretation of a classical (Greek Revival) theme, wherein the members forming the colonnade are simply rendered as square stone columns. This type of architecture is extremely effective and bows to no particular precedent, being merely a fine statement of what an all-masonry building can be when logically expressed.

ADRIAN VAN SINDEREN RESIDENCE   70 Willow Street. Built by a family that has lived on Brooklyn Heights for many years, this Greek Revival house boasts an elegant curved staircase with a classic niche above it. There is a beautiful private garden at the back.

FIRST UNITARIAN CHURCH Northeast corner Pierrepont Street and Monroe Place. This church, formerly known as the Church of the Saviour, is located on one of the widest and shortest streets in Brooklyn. With its high central gable and pointed windows flanked by small pinnacles, it has the true verticality of the Gothic Revival.

COLONNADED ROW HOUSES 43–49 Willow Place. Collectively impressive, these very small two-story houses would have had a mean, undistinguished appearance had they not been united by their colonnade. This was an early instance of town planning and was doubtless inspired by Underhill's grander Greek Revival colonnade — long since vanished — on Brooklyn Heights overlooking the harbor.

GRACE (Protestant Episcopal) **CHURCH** Southwest corner Hicks Street and Grace Court.
Located in a quiet backwater of the most fashionable section of the Heights, this Gothic
church is unusually low, long, and narrow. However, the nave and side aisles, spanned
by trusses, are well suited to the Episcopal service. The apse is well expressed on the exterior, and its traceried window is a prominent feature of the east end.

GREEN-WOOD CEMETERY GATES Fifth Avenue and 25th Street. One of the most splendid monuments of Brooklyn, this unique entrance to the cemetery combines offices, gates, a clock tower, and a spire in one imposing structure. It was designed by Richard Michell Upjohn, the son of the leading architect of the Gothic tradition in New York. The younger Upjohn also designed the Connecticut State Capitol at Hartford.

KINGS COUNTY SAVINGS BANK   Northeast corner Broadway and Bedford Avenue. Post–Civil War elegance in this country always aped the grandeur of Second Empire Paris. This bank, with its high mansard roofs, quoins in the walls, and rusticated first floor, was no exception.

WILLIAMSBURGH SAVINGS BANK Northwest corner Broadway and Driggs Avenue. After the Greek Revival, very few purely classical buildings were erected until the World's Columbian Exposition rearoused interest in the beauties of the ancient world. This Classic building, erected in 1875, is one of the few, and must have seemed imposing to a city of brownstone, brick, and Ruskinian polychromy.

EMMANUEL BAPTIST CHURCH   Northwest corner Lafayette Avenue and Saint James Place. Inspired by French Gothic prototypes, this large church, with its twin towers, resembles a small cathedral. Yet the interior is novel in arrangement, with a semicircular seating arrangement focused on the large baptismal font.

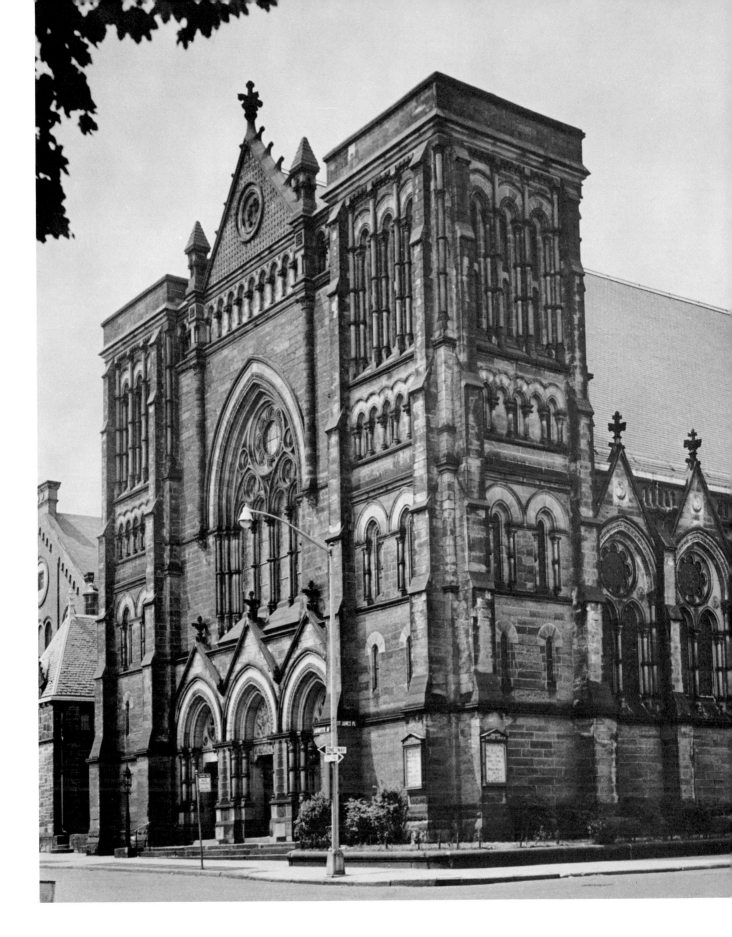

FRANKLIN TRUST BUILDING Southwest corner Montague and Clinton streets. This perfect little Romanesque skyscraper, complete with tile roofs and dormers, represented the epitome of style and success when it was built in the 'eighties. It was made possible by the elevator; and, in its verticality of expression, it was a direct forerunner of the Commercial Gothic skyscraper. The tower of Holy Trinity Church, at the right, frames this view.

MAIN POST OFFICE Johnson Street between Washington and Adams streets. After the Civil War, the federal government attempted to establish a new high standard of architecture in its buildings. The work was done by the Supervising Architect under the Treasury Department. This post office was built when Mifflin E. Bell was Supervising Architect; it represents a curious combination of French Renaissance and Romanesque Revival forms, to which are added certain German Renaissance details.

MONTAUK CLUB   Northeast corner Lincoln Place and Eighth Avenue at Grand Army Plaza. This club found its inspiration in the Ca d'Oro at Venice. It is built of brick and terra cotta, and a warm yellow color pervades the whole. Certain windows, reminiscent of the loggia of this Italian palazzo, are replete with flamboyant Venetian Gothic detail.

OLD BROOKLYN FIRE HEADQUARTERS 365 Jay Street. The culmination of the Romanesque Revival in New York was probably achieved in this little firehouse by Frank Freeman. As in all of his works, we see the skillful combination of elements; the beautiful colors of brick, brownstone, and copper; and the delicacy of the Romanesque ornament which, though not always archaeologically correct, is still extremely beautiful and expressive.

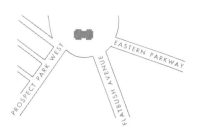

SOLDIERS AND SAILORS MEMORIAL ARCH   Grand Army Plaza. This full-fledged triumphal arch bearing aloft a sculptured quadriga is a symbol of civic pride as well as a memorial to the soldiers and sailors it honors. It marks the principal entrance to Brooklyn's most beautiful park and closes the long vista of Flatbush Avenue most effectively.

TO THE DEFENDERS OF THE UNION 1861-1865

ALL TRAFFIC →

CHARLES MILLARD PRATT RESIDENCE 241 Clinton Avenue. How truly comfortable and homelike a Romanesque Revival residence could be is well exemplified by this large house with its warm-colored brick and carved stonework, still maintained much as it was when built.

BROOKLYN SAVINGS BANK   Northeast corner Clinton and Pierrepont streets. This bank commands immediate attention with its skillful massing, beautiful fenestration, and imposing entrance door. When we enter this rectangular building, the large oval banking room comes as a complete surprise, but it is functionally effective and is ingeniously reconciled to its rectilinear enclosure. Frank Freeman, champion of the Romanesque Revival, was the architect. It was built in 1893, the year of the World's Columbian Exposition in Chicago.

VAN CORTLANDT MANOR Van Cortlandt Park. An excellent example of how the landed gentry lived in the eighteenth century in and about New York is this ample stone house with its wood shutters and unpretentious exterior, contrasting strangely with its rich Georgian interior. It is interesting to note that stone was widely used for country houses but rarely in the city, where brick predominated.

BARTOW MANSION Shore Road, Pelham Bay Park. French windows and a classic niche on the garden side of this stone house would lead us to believe that it was Italian in inspiration. However, the interior detail is Greek Revival, while the rather conventional front could almost be Georgian. This house has a timeless quality and is an extremely sophisticated piece of design for its day. The gardens are beautifully laid out in relation to the house, which is now the headquarters of the International Garden Club.

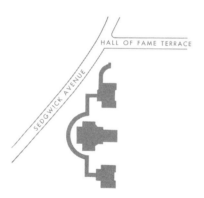

HALL OF FAME TERRACE

SEDGWICK AVENUE

HALL OF FAME, NEW YORK UNIVERSITY   University Avenue at West 181st Street. Surrounding the library building is this semicircular open-air colonnade known as the Hall of Fame, in which are displayed busts of famous men. As seen from below, this peculiarly Roman conceit provides an effective setting for the busts that it encloses. McKim, Mead & White were the architects.

LENT HOMESTEAD 7805 Nineteenth Road, Steinway. The beauty of this simple Dutch farm-house lies in its stonework and plain roof lines. Here we see how the seventeenth-century farmer built as best he might with the materials at hand — stone from the fields and roughhewn timbers and siding.

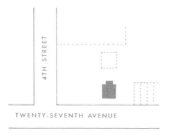

TWENTY-SEVENTH AVENUE HOUSE 417 Twenty-seventh Avenue, Astoria. Although the capitals of the columns are missing, this large house with its tetrastyle porch is a good example of the handsome architecture produced by the Greek Revival, in which an otherwise ordinary rectangular house might acquire both elegance and a certain degree of distinction through the addition of such a porch.

43RD AVENUE

VERNON BOULEVARD

43RD ROAD

BODINE CASTLE   43–16 Vernon Boulevard, Long Island City. With its rather gloomy, forbidding exterior implying Gothic origins, there is almost as much of the Romanesque in this "castle." It may be sensed primarily in the massing of the elements and in the round-arched windows and doors. In its present location in a lumber yard, it is difficult to visualize the spacious grounds and lawns that must have once surrounded this house.

BILLOPP (CONFERENCE) HOUSE Hylan Boulevard and Satterlee Street, Tottenville. Here
Christopher Billopp established "the Manor of Bentley," which later became Tottenville, on
the basis of a grant of land made to him by King James II in 1676. He built the house
toward the end of the century. His grandson, a Tory, entertained General Howe and his staff
here during the Revolution. This was the occasion of the "conference" held in the house in
1776, when Howe received Benjamin Franklin and John Adams, delegates from the Continental Congress, to see if a peace could be arranged. The conference proved abortive and
the delegates left under guard but unharmed.

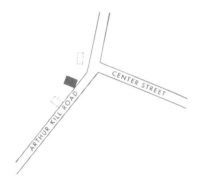

VOORLEZER'S HOUSE   Arthur Kill Road opposite Center Street, Richmondtown. This simple late-seventeenth-century house of the Dutch schoolteacher exists today to tell its story, thanks to the efforts of the Staten Island Historical Society and the Richmondtown Restoration now in progress.

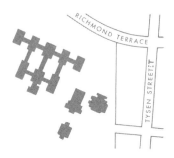

SAILORS' SNUG HARBOR   Richmond Terrace, New Brighton. Captain Randall's bequest endowing a home for retired seamen brought forth this grandiose group of buildings in Greek Revival style, the fashion of the day. Such results were rarely achieved. We are reminded of Stephen Girard's home and school for orphans, Girard College in Philadelphia.

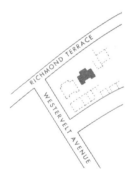

COLUMBIA HALL 404 Richmond Terrace, New Brighton. In character with the nearby Sailors' Snug Harbor, this Greek Revival building is a good example of the free manner in which a seemingly symmetrical building could conceal an asymmetrically planned house. The hexastyle Doric portico, though it reveals only one story, actually masks a second story behind the pediment.

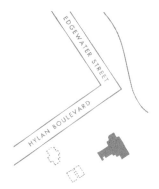

AUSTEN HOUSE 2 Hylan Boulevard, Rosebank. Staten Island was once the site of many rural villas, of which this was one of the most charming. It is an L-shaped house, one wing dating from the late seventeenth century and the other, overlooking the Narrows, from the eighteen-fifties. Legend has it that the newer wing, in Gothic Revival style, was designed by James Renwick, Jr., architect of Grace Church and friend of the Austen family.

(BEDLOE'S ISLAND)

LIBERTY ISLAND

THE STATUE OF LIBERTY Liberty (Bedloe's) Island, New York Harbor. This gift to the people of the United States from the French people is magnificently situated at the "sunset gates" of the harbor. It is superimposed on an island, a star fort (Fort Wood), and a base especially designed for it in monumental Neo-Grec by Richard Morris Hunt. The statue itself was conceived by the French sculptor Auguste Bartholdi, and the engineering for the frame which supports it was done by Gustave Eiffel, designer of the Eiffel Tower in Paris.

VIII. INDEX OF ARCHITECTURALLY NOTABLE STRUCTURES IN GREATER NEW YORK

INTRODUCTORY

T HE following index of buildings has been approved by the Committee on Historic Architecture of the Municipal Art Society and submitted to the Committee on Landmarks for inclusion in this book. It consists of buildings built before 1930, within the five boroughs of Greater New York, which are considered worthy of preservation for their architectural distinction, without consideration for their historical associations. The buildings have been classified in categories as indicated below, with a code to special features.

It is recognized that no index of buildings, such as that which follows, can ever be completely correct. The Society has taken the precaution of having a "verification sheet" made for every structure entered in this index, to insure that the information contained here be as accurate as possible.

The Municipal Art Society and the individuals connected with this work assume no legal responsibility for the completeness or accuracy of the information contained herein, nor for the appreciation or depreciation in value of any of the premises listed herein, by reason of their inclusion in this index.

Photograph of a typical plaque placed on a building by
The New York Community Trust

CATEGORY CLASSIFICATION OF BUILDINGS IN GREATER NEW YORK DESIGNATED WORTHY OF PRESERVATION

Category

I. Structures of national importance which should be preserved at all costs.

II. Structures of great local or regional importance which should be preserved.

III. Structures of importance designated for preservation.

"F." Structures of note filed for ready reference.

Code to Special Features

c. Community picture

g. Stained glass

h. Historical interest

i. Iron or other metalwork

l. Landscaping and civic planning

m. Mosaics

o. Architectural ornament

p. Mural paintings

s. Sculpture incorporated in the design

BOROUGH OF MANHATTAN

Buildings in Manhattan Built Before 1930

CATEGORY I. Structures of national importance which should be preserved at all costs

STRUCTURE	ARCHITECT	DATE	STYLE	CODE
Castle Clinton National Monument *Battery Park*	Col. Jonathan Williams and John McComb, Jr.	1808–11	Military	H.
*Dyckman House *Broadway at West 204th St.*	William Dyckman, owner-builder	c.1783	Dutch Colonial	H.
Restored	Alexander M. Welch	1915		
Federal Hall National Memorial (formerly U.S. Subtreasury) *N.E. cor. Wall and Nassau sts.*	Town and Davis, S. Thomson and Frazee	1834–42	Greek Revival	C.H.I.O.
*Grace Church *N.E. cor. Broadway and East 10th St.*	James Renwick, Jr.	1843–46	Gothic Revival	C.G.H.S.
Morgan Library *29 East 36th St.*	McKim, Mead & White	1905–06	Italian Renaissance Eclectic	O.P.S.
Annex	Benjamin W. Morris	1927–28		
New York City Hall *Broadway at City Hall Park*	Mangin and McComb	1803–12	Federal (French influence)	C.H.O.
Restoration	Grosvenor Atterbury	1908–15		
*St. Paul's Chapel *Broadway between Fulton and Vesey sts.*	Thomas McBean	1764–66	Georgian	C.G.H.S.
Steeple	James C. Lawrence	1793–94		

* Asterisk indicates that a plaque has been placed on the building by the New York Community Trust.

STRUCTURE	ARCHITECT	DATE	STYLE	CODE
Statue of Liberty *Liberty Island* (*Bedloe's Island*)	Frédéric Bartholdi, sculptor Gustave Eiffel, engineer	1883–84		C.H.S.
Base	Richard M. Hunt General Stone, engineer		Neo-Grec	
*Trinity Church *Broadway opposite Wall St.*	Richard Upjohn	1840–46	Gothic Revival	C.G.H.S.

CATEGORY II. Structures of great local or regional importance which should be preserved

NOTE: Two entire areas of Manhattan — Greenwich Village and Gramercy Park — are worthy of classification in Category II. These areas have more importance for the community picture than for the intrinsic merit of each structure.

Churches

STRUCTURE	ARCHITECT	DATE	STYLE	CODE
*Cathedral Church of St. John the Divine *Amsterdam Ave. and Morningside Dr., 110th–113th Sts.*				
Choir, apse, and original crossing	Heins and LaFarge (won in competition)	1892–1907	Romanesque Eclectic	G.I.M. O.S.
Nave, final crossing, and transept	Cram & Ferguson	After 1911	French Gothic Eclectic	
*Church of the Ascension *N.W. cor. Fifth Ave. and West 10th St.*	Richard Upjohn	1840–41	Gothic Revival	G.P.S.
Interior decorated by	John LaFarge, A. Saint-Gaudens, and Stanford White	1885–89		
Friends' Meeting House *221 East 15th St.* (*Stuyvesant Square*)	Charles T. Bunting	1860	Colonial Survival	C.H.
*Mission of Our Lady of the Rosary (Watson House) *7 State St.*	Unknown	c.1800	Federal	H.O.
East portion		c.1793	Federal	H.O.
West wing (colonnaded)		1805		

STRUCTURE	ARCHITECT	DATE	STYLE	CODE
St. Marks-in-the-Bouwerie *N.W. cor. Stuyvesant St. and Second Ave.*	Unknown	1795–99	Georgian	C.G.H.S.
Steeple	Martin E. Thompson	c.1828	Greek Revival	
Stone portico and additions at rear		1835–36		
Cast-iron portico		1858	Italianate	I.
St. Martin's (P.E.) Church (formerly Church of the Holy Trinity) *S.E. cor. Lenox Ave. and West 122nd St.*	William A. Potter	1888	Romanesque Revival	O.
St. Patrick's (R.C.) Cathedral *Fifth and Madison aves. between East 50th and 51st sts.*	James Renwick, Jr.	1858–79	Gothic Revival	O.S.
Lady Chapel *Madison Ave.*	Charles T. Matthews	1906	French Gothic Eclectic	O.S.
St. Peter's (R.C.) Church *S.E. cor. Barclay and Church sts.*	Attributed to Isaiah Rogers	1836–40	Greek Revival	H.
*St. Thomas' Church *N.W. cor. Fifth Ave. and West 53rd St.*	Cram, Goodhue & Ferguson	1906–10	French Gothic Eclectic	G.O.S.
Reredos	B. G. Goodhue	1918		
Bells	Mayers, Murray and Phillip	1929		

Public Buildings and Monuments

*American Museum of Natural History *Central Park West and West 77th St.*				
Original portion	Vaux and Mould	1874–77	Victorian Gothic	
77th St. façade	J. C. Cady & Co.	c.1890	Romanesque Revival	O.
Roosevelt Memorial (*C.P.W.*)	John Russell Pope	1929–36	Roman Eclectic	O.S.
Equestrian statue of Theodore Roosevelt	James E. Fraser			

STRUCTURE	ARCHITECT	DATE	STYLE	CODE
The Arsenal *Central Park* *Fifth Ave. at 64th St.*	Martin E. Thompson	1847–48	Military	H.P.
Alterations	Richard M. Hunt	1860	Military	
Bethesda Fountain	Emma Stebbins, sculptor	1873	Victorian Gothic	C.I.S.
Esplanade *Central Park*	Vaux and Mould, architects	c.1864	Victorian Gothic	O.
Brooklyn Bridge *City Hall Square to* *Parkes Cadman Plaza*	John A. Roebling Washington A. Roebling	1867–69 1869–83	Modified Gothic Revival	C.H.I.
Farragut Monument *Madison Square, north-* *east corner*	A. Saint-Gaudens, sculptor	1880–81	Proto-Art-Nouveau	S.
Base	Stanford White, architect			O.
General Grant National Memorial *Riverside Dr. at West* *122nd St.*	John H. Duncan	1892–97	Classic Eclectic	C.H.L.
Restored	Aymar Embury, II	c.1939		
Grand Army Plaza *Fifth Ave., 59th–60th sts.*	Olmsted and Vaux	1858–65		
Statue of General William Tecumseh Sherman	A. Saint-Gaudens	1903		S.
Pulitzer Fountain	Thomas Hastings	1916	Italian Renaissance Eclectic	C.L.S.
Sculpture of figure "Abundance"	Karl Bitter	1916		S.
*Jefferson Market Court-house *S.W. cor. Sixth Ave. and* *West 10th St.*	Withers and Vaux	1874–77	Victorian Gothic	C.G.I. O.S.
Low Library Columbia University *West 116th St.*	McKim, Mead & White	1893–97	Roman Eclectic	C.H.
Metropolitan Museum of Art, Central Portion *Fifth Ave. at 82nd St.*	Richard M. Hunt (Richard H. Hunt completed work)	1894–95 1895–1902	Roman Eclectic	O.S.
New York County Lawyers Association *14 Vesey St.*	Cass Gilbert	1930	Federal Eclectic	O.

STRUCTURE	ARCHITECT	DATE	STYLE	CODE
New York Public Library *Fifth Ave., 40th–42nd sts.*	Carrère and Hastings	1902–09	Beaux Arts Eclectic	L.O.S.
Figures above fountains	Frederick MacMonnies	c.1920		
Lions	E. C. Potter	1911		
*New York Stock Exchange *Broad and Wall sts.*	George B. Post	1901–04	Beaux Arts Eclectic	O.S.
Pediment group	J. Q. A. Ward assisted by Paul W. Bartlett, sculptors			
Old Assay Office Building Façade *American Wing* *Metropolitan Museum of* *Art*	Martin E. Thompson	1823	Federal	H.O.
Pennsylvania Station *Seventh and Eighth aves.* *betw. 31st and 33rd sts.*	McKim, Mead & White	1906–10	Roman Eclectic	C.O.P.S.
Seventy-First Regiment Armory *S.E. cor. Park Ave. and* *East 34th St.*	Clinton and Russell	1904–06	Military	C.O.
U.S. Federal Reserve Bank *Liberty St. and Maiden* *Lane betw. Nassau and* *William sts.*	York & Sawyer	1928	Italian Renaissance Eclectic	C.I.
Washington Arch *Fifth Ave. at Washington* *Square*	Stanford White	1889–92	Modified Roman Eclectic	C.O.S.
In war	Herman A. MacNeil, sculptor	1916		
In peace	Stirling Calder, sculptor	1918		
Watchtower (cast-iron) *Mount Morris Park,* *opposite East 121st St.*	Attributed to James Bogardus, engineer-designer	c.1855	Classic Revival	C.I.

Hotels and Clubs

*Association of the Bar of the City of New York *42 West 44th St.*	Cyrus L. W. Eidlitz	1895–97	Classic Eclectic	O.

STRUCTURE	ARCHITECT	DATE	STYLE	CODE
Century Association (Club) *7 West 43rd St.*	McKim, Mead & White	1889–91	Italian Renaissance Eclectic	O.
*Harvard Club *27 West 44th St.* Extensions *West 45th St.*	McKim, Mead & White	1894	Georgian Eclectic	O.
Harvard Hall		1902–05	Italian Renaissance Eclectic	O.
Main Dining Room		1914–15	Modified Georgian Eclectic	
Metropolitan Club *N.E. cor. Fifth Ave. and East 60th St.*	McKim, Mead & White	1892–94	Italian Renaissance Eclectic	I.O.
East wing fifth floor	Ogden Codman, Jr.	1912	Italian Renaissance Eclectic	
Colonnade relocated	McKim, Mead & White	1922		
Plaza Hotel *Central Park South and Fifth Ave.*	Henry J. Hardenbergh	1906–07	French Renaissance Eclectic	C.
Racquet and Tennis Club *Park Ave. between East 52nd and 53rd sts.*	McKim, Mead & White	1916–18	Italian Renaissance Eclectic	O.
*University Club *N.W. cor. Fifth Ave. and West 54th St.*	McKim, Mead & White	1897–1900	Italian Renaissance Eclectic	O.P.

Commercial Buildings

STRUCTURE	ARCHITECT	DATE	STYLE	CODE
American Telephone and Telegraph Building *S.W. cor. Broadway and Fulton St.*	William Welles Bosworth	1913	Roman Eclectic	S.I.
Additions		1916, 1922		
Bayard (Condict) Building *65–69 Bleecker St.*	Louis Sullivan Lyndon P. Smith (supervising architect)	1897–99	Sullivanian	H.O.S.
Black, Starr, & Frost *S.W. cor. Fifth Ave. and West 48th St.*	Carrère and Hastings	1911–12	Italian Renaissance Eclectic	O.S.
Cast–iron building *N.W. cor. Washington and Murray sts.*	James Bogardus	1848	Classic Revival	H.I.O.

STRUCTURE	ARCHITECT	DATE	STYLE	CODE
DeVinne Press Building *N.E. cor. Lafayette and East 4th sts.*	Babb, Cook & Willard	1885–86	Romanesque Revival	I.O.
*Metropolitan Life Tower *S.E. cor. East 24th St. and Madison Ave. (Madison Square)*	N. LeBrun and Sons	1908–09	Italian Renaissance Eclectic	O.
Remodeled	Lloyd Morgan	1962		
Singer Building *N.W. cor. Broadway and Liberty St.*	Ernest Flagg	1897–98	Beaux Arts Eclectic	I.O.
Tower and addition	Ernest Flagg	1906–08	Beaux Arts Eclectic	
*Woolworth Building *Broadway between Park Place and Barclay St.*	Cass Gilbert	1911–13	Gothic Eclectic	C.O.

Houses and Apartments

STRUCTURE	ARCHITECT	DATE	STYLE	CODE
Colonnade Row (LaGrange Terrace) *428–434 Lafayette St.*	A. J. Davis (Seth Geer)	1836	Classic Revival	C.H.
*Dakota Apartments *Central Park West between West 72nd and 73rd sts.*	Henry J. Hardenbergh	1882–84	German Renaissance Eclectic	C.I.O.
Frick Mansion (Frick Museum) *Fifth Ave. between East 70th and 71st sts.*	Carrère and Hastings	1913–14	French Classic Eclectic (Louis XVI)	L.O.S.
Library and other additions	John R. Pope	1931–35		
*Gracie Mansion *Carl Schurz Park East End Ave. at East 88th St.*	Unknown (built for Archibald Gracie)	c.1799	Federal	H.
Hamilton Grange *Convent Ave., 141st and 142nd sts.*	John McComb, Jr.	1802	Federal	H.
*Morris–Jumel House *West 160th St. and Jumel Terrace*	Unknown	c.1765	Georgian	H.O.

STRUCTURE	ARCHITECT	DATE	STYLE	CODE
"Old Merchant's House" (Seabury Tredwell res.) *29 East 4th St.*	Influence of Minard Lafever	1832	Greek Revival (transitional)	H.O.
George F. Baker res. *N.W. cor. East 93 St. and Park Ave.*	Delano and Aldrich	1917	Federal Eclectic	O.
Enlarged		1928–29		
Villard Mansion *Madison Ave. between East 50th and 51st sts.*	McKim, Mead & White	1884–85	Italian Renaissance Eclectic	C.I.M. P.S.
Washington Square houses, nos. 19–26 *North side of Square west of Fifth Ave.*	Unknown	c.1830	Greek Revival	C.

CATEGORY III. Structures of importance designated for preservation

Churches

*Central Synagogue *S.W. cor. Lexington Ave. and East 55th St.*	Henry Fernbach	1872	Moorish Revival	O.
Church of the Heavenly Rest *S.E. cor. East 90th St. and Fifth Ave.*	Mayers, Murray and Phillip B. G. Goodhue, associate	1927–29	French Gothic Eclectic	G.S.
*Church of the Holy Communion *N.E. cor. Sixth Ave. and West 20th St.*	Richard Upjohn	1844–46	Gothic Revival	C.
*Church of St. Ignatius Loyola *S.W. cor. Park Ave. and East 84th St.*	Schickel & Ditmars	1898–99	Italian Renaissance Eclectic	O.
*Church of St. Vincent Ferrer *S.E. cor. Lexington Ave. and East 66th St.*	B. G. Goodhue Lee Lawrie, sculptor	1915–18	French Gothic Eclectic	G.I.O.S.

STRUCTURE	ARCHITECT	DATE	STYLE	CODE
*Church of St. Paul the Apostle *Columbus Ave. between West 59th and 60th sts.*	Jeremiah O'Rourke (completed by Fr. Deshon)	1876–85	Gothic Revival (late)	G.M.P.S.
Altar and Baldachino Angels	Stanford White F. MacMonnies, sculptor	1889	Italian Renaissance Eclectic	
Windows in Chancel	John LaFarge	1888		
*Church Missions' House *S.E. cor. East 22nd St. and Fourth Ave.*	R. W. Gibson Edward J. N. Stent	1892–94	Romanesque Eclectic	O.S.
First Presbyterian Church *Fifth Ave. between West 11th and 12th sts.*	Joseph C. Wells	1844–46	Gothic Revival	C.G.O.
Friends' Meeting House *144 East 20th St.*	King and Kellum	1859–60	Italianate	C.
*West Building, General Theological Seminary *Ninth Ave. and West 20th St.*	Unknown	1834–36	Gothic Revival	C.
John Street M.E. Church *44 John St.*	Unknown	Founded 1768 Rebuilt 1817, 1841	Late Georgian	H.
Judson Memorial Church *S.W. cor. Washington Square South and Thompson St.*	McKim, Mead & White	1890–93	Italian Renaissance Eclectic	C.G.I. O.S.
Marble Collegiate Church *N.W. cor. Fifth Ave. and West 29th St.*	Samuel A. Warner	1851–54	Romanesque Revival	C.
Mariners' Temple *Oliver and Henry sts.*	Attributed to Minard Lafever	1844	Greek Revival	C.
*Park Avenue Christian Church *S.W. cor. Park Avenue and East 85th St.*	Cram, Goodhue & Ferguson	1909–11	Gothic Eclectic	G.O.

STRUCTURE	ARCHITECT	DATE	STYLE	CODE
St. Augustine's Chapel (formerly All Saints Church) *S.E. cor. Henry and Scammel sts.*	Attributed to John Heath	1827	Georgian-Gothic	C.
St. Bartholomew's Church *Park Ave. between East 50th and 51st sts.*	B. G. Goodhue	1917–23	Modified Byzantine Eclectic	C.G.M.S.
Completed with dome and Chapter House	Mayers, Murray and Phillip	1926–27		
Entrance Portico [moved from Madison Ave.]	McKim, Mead & White	c.1902–03	Romanesque Eclectic	O.S.
Doors: Center	Daniel C. French			
North	Philip Martiny			
South	Herbert Adams			
Angel Font	Thorwaldsen			
Mosaics	Hildreth Meière			
St. George's Church *Stuyvesant Square (West)*	Blesch and Eidlitz	1846–48	Modified Romanesque Revival	C.H.
Rebuilt	Leopold Eidlitz	1865–67		
Parish House *207 East 16th St.*	Leopold Eidlitz	1887	Romanesque Revival	O.
Centennial Chapel (adjoining church)	M. L. and H. G. Emery	1911–12	Romanesque Eclectic	O.
*St. James' Church *St. James St. nr. Chatham Square*	Attributed to Minard Lafever	1835–37	Greek Revival	O.
St. John's in the Village *S.W. cor. Waverly Place and West 11th St.*	Unknown	1846	Greek Revival	
St. Joseph's (R.C.) Church *Sixth Ave. at Waverly Place*	Unknown	1833	Greek Revival	O.
St. Patrick's (R.C.) Church (former cathedral) *S.W. cor. Mott and Prince sts.*	Doyle and Mangin	1809–15	Gothic Revival	H.
Rebuilt		1866		
*St. Peter's Episcopal Church *346 West 20th St.*	James W. Smith, builder, after designs by Clement C. Moore	1836–38	Gothic Revival	C.O.

STRUCTURE	ARCHITECT	DATE	STYLE	CODE
*Sea and Land Church *S.W. cor. Henry and* *Market sts.*	Unknown	1817–19	Georgian- Gothic	H.
*Spring Street Church *250 Spring St.*	Unknown	1835–36	Greek Revival	

Public Buildings and Monuments

STRUCTURE	ARCHITECT	DATE	STYLE	CODE
*Academy of Medicine *2 East 103rd St.*	York & Sawyer	1925–26	Romanesque Eclectic	O.
*American Fine Arts Society *215 West 57th St.*	Henry J. Hardenbergh Hunting and Jacobsen	1892	French Renais- sance Eclectic	O.
Appellate Division of the Supreme Court of N.Y. *N.E. cor. Madison Ave. and* *East 25th St.*	James Brown Lord	1900	Classic Eclectic	O.P.S.
Astor Library (old) (Hebrew Sheltering and Immigrant Aid Society) *425 Lafayette St.*				
Central portion	Alexander Saeltzer	1859	Romanesque Revival (early)	I.
Wings	North: Thomas Stent South: Griffith Thomas	1881		
Chamber of Commerce Building *65 Liberty St.*	James B. Baker	1901–02	Beaux Arts Eclectic	O.P.S.
*Cooper Union *Cooper Square and* *Astor Place*	Frederic A. Peterson	1859	Italianate	C.H.
Columbus Circle *West 59th St., Eighth Ave.,* *and Broadway*				C.L.S.
(for space-planning and monuments) Columbus Monument	Gaetano Russo, sculptor	1892	Classic Eclectic	
Merchants' Gate to Central Park with Maine Monument *Central Park West at* *West 59th St.*	H. Van Buren Magonigle, architect Attilio Piccirilli, sculptor	1901–13	Beaux Arts Eclectic	O.S.

STRUCTURE	ARCHITECT	DATE	STYLE	CODE
Grand Central Terminal *East 42nd St. between Vanderbilt and Lexington aves.*	Warren and Wetmore Reed and Stem Col. Wm. J. Wilgus, engineer	1903–13	Beaux Arts Eclectic	C.I.O.S.
Metropolitan Opera House *Broadway at West 40th St.*	J. Cleveland Cady	1883	Modified Italian Renaissance Eclectic	C.H.
Auditorium (rebuilt)	Carrère and Hastings	1893	French Classic Eclectic (Louis XIV)	
Public Baths *N.E. cor. East 23rd St. and Asser Levy Place*	Arnold W. Brunner and W. Martin Aiken	1904–06	Roman Eclectic	C.L.
Riverside Drive Embankments, terraces, pergolas, etc.	Frederick L. Olmsted, landscape architect	c.1909	Classic Eclectic	C.L.
Iron and stone bridges *Central Park*	Vaux and Mould	c.1860	Victorian Gothic	I.L.O.
*Seventh Regiment Armory *Park and Lexington aves. between East 66th and 67th sts.*	Clinton and Russell Charles MacDonald, engineer	1877–80	Military Neo-Grec	I.O.
Soldiers and Sailors Monument *Riverside Drive at West 89th St.*	Charles W. and Arthur A. Stoughton Paul Duboy, sculptor	1900–02	Beaux Arts Eclectic	C.L.O.
United States Customs House *Bowling Green*	Cass Gilbert	1901–07	Beaux Arts Eclectic	I.O.P.S.
Sculptured figures at north façade	Daniel C. French			
Vanderbilt Gates [*Moved to*] *Fifth Ave. and 110th St.*	George B. Post	1894	French Classic Eclectic (Louis XIV)	I.
Water Tower at High Bridge *Amsterdam Ave. and Harlem River*	Croton Aqueduct Dept., engineer	c.1848	Modified Gothic Revival	C.H.

Hotels and Clubs

STRUCTURE	ARCHITECT	DATE	STYLE	CODE
Fraunces Tavern (Stephen DeLancey residence) *Broad and Pearl sts.*	Unknown	c.1700	Georgian	C.H.
Remodeled	William H. Mersereau	1905–07	Georgian Eclectic	

STRUCTURE	ARCHITECT	DATE	STYLE	CODE
Gotham Hotel *S.W. cor. Fifth Ave.* *and West 55th St.*	Hiss and Weekes	1902–05	Beaux Arts Eclectic	
India House *Hanover Square*	Unknown	c.1837	Classic Revival	H.
Interior remodeled Exterior restoration	Delano and Aldrich Herbert Wheeler	1924–25 1951		O.
*Knickerbocker Club *S.E. cor. Fifth Ave. and* *East 62nd St.*	Delano and Aldrich	1914–15	Federal Eclectic	O.P.
*Lotos Club (formerly Schieffelin residence) *5 East 66th St.*	Richard H. Hunt	1898–1900	Beaux Arts Eclectic	
Manhattan Club (American Jockey Club) *Madison Square* *S.E. cor. Madison Ave. and* *East 26th St.*	Thomas R. Jackson	1866	French influence (Second Empire)	C.
*National Arts Club (former residence of S. J. Tilden) *15 Gramercy Park South*	Vaux & Radford	1871–74	Victorian Gothic	G.H.O.S.
New York Yacht Club *37 West 44th St.*	Warren and Wetmore	1899	Beaux Arts Eclectic	O.S.
*The Players (Club) (former residence of Valentine Hall, occupied by Edwin Booth in 1888) *16 Gramercy Park South*	Unknown	1850's	Gothic Revival	
Converted into club Entrance portico	Stanford White of McKim, Mead & White	1892	Italian Renais- sance Eclectic	H.I.
St. Regis Hotel *S.E. cor. Fifth Ave.* *and East 55th St.*	Trowbridge and Livingston	1901–04	Beaux Arts Eclectic	I.O.
*Salmagundi Club *47 Fifth Ave.*	Unknown	c.1850	Italianate	
Shelton Hotel *S.E. cor. Lexington Ave.* *and East 49th St.*	Arthur Loomis Harmon	1922–24	Romanesque Eclectic	O.

STRUCTURE	ARCHITECT	DATE	STYLE	CODE
*Bowery Savings Bank *110 East 42nd St.*	York & Sawyer	1921–23	Romanesque Eclectic	M.S.O.
Bush Terminal Building *130 West 42nd St.*	Helmle and Corbett	1918	Gothic Eclectic	O.
*East River Savings Bank *N.E. cor. West 96th St. and Amsterdam Ave.*	Walker and Gillette	1926–27	Classic Eclectic	O.
Evening Post Building (old) *20 Vesey St.*	Robert D. Kohn	1906	Art Nouveau	O.S.
*First National City Bank *55 Wall St.* (originally Merchants' Exchange, later U.S. Customs House)	Isaiah Rogers	1836–42	Greek Revival	H.
Alterations for Bank	McKim, Mead & White	1907–09		
Flatiron Building (Fuller Building) *Broadway at East 23rd St. and Fifth Ave.*	D. H. Burnham & Co.	1901–03	Renaissance Eclectic	C.H.
Franklin Savings Bank *S.E. cor. Eighth Ave. and West 42nd St.*	York & Sawyer	1899	Beaux Arts Eclectic	O.
Gorham Building *S.W. cor. Fifth Ave. and West 36th St.*	McKim, Mead & White	1903–05	Italian Renaissance Eclectic	O.
*Greenwich Savings Bank *West 36th St. between Sixth Ave. and Broadway*	York and Sawyer	1922–24	Classic Eclectic	
E. V. Haughwout & Co. *N.E. cor. Broadway and Broome St.*	J. P. Gaynor	1857	Italianate	H.I.O.
Lord and Taylor (former building) *S.W. cor. Broadway and West 20th St.*	J. H. Giles	1869–70	French influence (Second Empire)	I.
McGraw-Hill Building *330 West 42nd St.*	Hood, Godley and Fouilhoux	1930	Horizontal Modern	
*Morgan Guaranty Trust *140 Broadway*	York and Sawyer	1911–13	Modified Roman Eclectic	

STRUCTURE	ARCHITECT	DATE	STYLE	CODE
*New York Daily News Building *220 East 42nd St.*	John Mead Howells and Raymond Hood	1930	Vertical Modern	
Rockefeller Center *Fifth to Sixth Aves.* *West 48th to 50th sts.* (as an example of comprehensive planning)	Reinhard and Hofmeister Corbett, Harrison and MacMurray Hood and Fouilhoux	1930–37	Vertical Modern	C.L.M. P.S.

Houses and Apartments

*The Apthorpe (apts.) *West End Ave. and* *Broadway, between West* *78th and 79th sts.*	Clinton and Russell	1906–08	Italian Renaissance Eclectic	C.O.
The Belnord (apts.) *Broadway and Amsterdam* *Ave. between West 86th* *and 87th sts.*	H. Hobart Weekes	1908	Renaissance Eclectic	C.O.
Carnegie Mansion (School for Social Research, Columbia University) *Fifth Ave. between East* *91st and 92nd sts.*	Babb, Cook & Willard	1899–1903	Modified Georgian Eclectic	C.
*Mrs. James B. Duke residence (Institute of Fine Arts, New York University) *N.E. cor. Fifth Ave. and* *East 78th St.*	Horace Trumbauer	1910–12	French Classic Eclectic (Louis XV)	C.O.
Gramercy Park *Numbers 3 and 4*	Unknown	c.1840	Modified Greek Revival	C.I.
Edward S. Harkness res. (Commonwealth Fund) *N.E. cor. Fifth Ave. and* *East 75th st.*	Hale and Rogers	1907	Italian Renaissance Eclectic	I.O.
William Starr Miller res. (Yivo Institute) *S.E. cor. Fifth Ave. and* *East 86th St.*	Carrère and Hastings	1912–14	French Classic Eclectic (Louis XIII)	O.
Theodore Roosevelt house *28 East 20th St.*	Unknown	c.1850	Gothic Revival	H.
Remodeled as a museum	Theodate Pope	1921–23		

STRUCTURE	ARCHITECT	DATE	STYLE	CODE
Abigail Adams Smith house (former carriage house) Colonial Dames of America Hq. *421 East 61st St.*	Unknown	1799	Vernacular Federal	C.H.
Felix M. Warburg residence (Jewish Museum) *N.E. cor. East 92nd St. and Fifth Ave.*	C. P. H. Gilbert	c.1908	French Renaissance Eclectic	O.
Mrs. Orme Wilson res. (India Consulate) *3 East 64th St.*	Warren and Wetmore	1900–03	Beaux Arts Eclectic	O.

CATEGORY "F." Structures of note filed for ready reference

Churches

STRUCTURE	ARCHITECT	DATE	STYLE	CODE
Christ Church *211 West 71st St.*	C. C. Haight	1889–90	Romanesque Revival	O.
*Church of the Holy Apostles *S.E. cor. Ninth Ave. and West 28th St.*	Attributed to Minard Lafever	1844–48	Modified Romanesque Revival	C.
Choir		1854		
Transepts	Babcock of R. Upjohn & Son	1858		
Restored	Kerr Rainsford	c.1925		
Church of the Holy Trinity (Rhinelander Memorial) *312 East 88th St.*	Barney and Chapman	1895–97	Gothic Eclectic	C.G.O.
Parish Buildings			French Renaissance Eclectic	O.
Church of the Incarnation *N.E. cor. Madison Ave. and East 35th St.*	Emlen T. Littell	1864–65	Modified Gothic Revival	M.P.

STRUCTURE	ARCHITECT	DATE	STYLE	CODE
*Church of the Transfiguration ("Little Church Around the Corner") *1 East 29th St.*	Unknown	1849–56	Gothic Revival	C.G.H.
Lich Gate	Frederick C. Withers	1896	Gothic Eclectic	C.
St. John's Evangelical Lutheran Church *81 Christopher St.*	Unknown	c.1821	Modified Federal	
*St. Luke's Chapel *483 Hudson St.*	Attributed to John Heath	1821	Vernacular Federal	C.H.
St. Paul's Chapel Columbia University *West 117th St. and Amsterdam Ave.*	Howells and Stokes	1904–07	Italian Renaissance Eclectic	O.
*Trinity Chapel (Serbian E. O. Cathedral of St. Sava) *21 West 25th St.*	Richard Upjohn	1852–55	Gothic Revival	O.
Village Presbyterian Church *143 West 13th St.*	Attributed to Samuel Thomson	1846	Greek Revival	
West End Collegiate Church and School *N.E. cor. West 77th St. and West End Ave.*	Robert W. Gibson	1891–92	Flemish Renaissance Eclectic	C.O.

Public Buildings

American Academy of Arts and Letters *633 West 155th St.*				
North Building	Cass Gilbert	1929–30	Classic Eclectic	L.
South Building	McKim, Mead & White	1921–22	Classic Eclectic	L.
American Geographic Society	Charles P. Huntington	1904–11	Classic Eclectic	L.
Hispanic Society		1905–08	Classic Eclectic	L.
American Numismatic Society		1907	Classic Eclectic	L.
Museum of the American Indian Gardens and Esplanade *Broadway at West 155th and 156th sts.*		1922	Classic Eclectic	L.

STRUCTURE	ARCHITECT	DATE	STYLE	CODE
Carnegie Hall *S.E. cor. Seventh Ave.* *and West 57th St.*	William B. Tuthill (Dankmar Adler, consultant on acoustics)	1889–91	Modified Italian Renaissance Eclectic	H.
Regis High School *East 84th–85th sts.* *between Park and Madison* *aves.*	Maginnis and Walsh	1913–17	Classic Eclectic	

Hotels and Clubs

Ansonia Hotel (apts.) *Broadway between West* *73rd and 74th sts.*	Graves and Duboy for W. E. D. Stokes	1899–1904	Beaux Arts Eclectic	C.O.
Chelsea Hotel *222 West 23rd St.*	Hubert, Pirrson & Co.	1883	Victorian Gothic	I.O.
Vanderbilt Hotel *Park Ave. between* *East 33rd and 34th sts.*	Warren and Wetmore	1910–12	Federal Eclectic (Adam influence)	O.

Commercial Buildings

American Radiator Building *40 West 40th St.*	Raymond Hood	1924	Vertical Modern	O.
American Surety Building *S.E. cor. Broadway and* *Pine St.*	Bruce Price	1894–96	Classic Eclectic	S.
*Cunard Building *Broadway at Morris St.*	Benjamin W. Morris	1919–21	Italian Renais- sance Eclectic	M.O.P.
Great Hall	Thomas Hastings			
Murals	Ezra Winter, painter			
Jones Speedometer Building *N.E. cor. Broadway and* *West 76th St.*	Oscar Lowinson	1906–07	Art Nouveau	O.
Metal Exchange Building (formerly Seventh Ward Bank) *S.E. cor. Pearl and John* *sts.*	Attributed to John B. Snook	c.1846–47	Classic Revival	H.
New York Telephone Co. Building *West St. between Vesey* *and Barclay sts.*	McKenzie, Voorhees and Gmelin	1923–27	Vertical Modern	O.

STRUCTURE	ARCHITECT	DATE	STYLE	CODE
Sun Building (first A. T. Stewart store) *N.E. cor. Broadway and Chambers St.*	John B. Snook	1844	Italianate	C.H.
*Tiffany and Co. garage *140 East 41st St.*	McKim, Mead & White	1904–05	Neo-Palladian Eclectic	
*Times Building *Times Square West 42nd St. between Broadway and Seventh Ave.*	Eidlitz and Mackenzie	1903	Italian Renaissance Eclectic	C.O.
Vincent Office Building *S.E. cor. Broadway and Duane St.*	George B. Post	1899	Romanesque Revival	O.

Houses and Apartments

Alwyn Court Apts. *S.E. cor. West 58th St. and Seventh Ave.*	Harde & Short	1907–08	French Renaissance Eclectic	O.
Isaac Vail Brokaw residence (Institute of Electrical & Electronics Engineers) *N.E. cor. East 79th St. and Fifth Ave.*	Rose and Stone	1887–88	French Renaissance Eclectic	C.O.
Henry P. Davison residence *S.W. cor. Park Ave. and East 69th St.*	Walker and Gillette	1916–17	Georgian Eclectic	O.
Otto Kahn residence (Convent of the Sacred Heart) *N.E. cor. Fifth Ave. and East 91st St.*	J. Armstrong Stenhouse	1916–19	Italian Renaissance Eclectic	O.
Percy R. Pyne residence *N.W. cor. Park Ave. and East 68th St.*	McKim, Mead & White	1909–11	Federal Eclectic	O.
Elihu Root residence *S.E. cor. Park Ave. and East 71st St.*	Carrère and Hastings	1903	Modified Federal Eclectic	
Sniffen Court Stables (remodeled as residences) *East 36th St. between Lexington and Third aves.*	Unknown	1850–60	Romanesque Revival (Early)	C.

STRUCTURE	ARCHITECT	DATE	STYLE	CODE
*James Stillman residence (formerly Henry T. Sloane residence) *9 East 72nd St.*	Carrère and Hastings	1894–96	Beaux Arts Eclectic	o.
Willard Straight residence (Audubon Society) *N.E. cor. Fifth Ave. and East 94th St.*	Delano and Aldrich	1913–15	Federal Eclectic	o.

BOROUGH OF BROOKLYN

Buildings in Brooklyn Built Before 1930

CATEGORY I. Structures of national importance which should be preserved at all costs

STRUCTURE	ARCHITECT	DATE	STYLE	CODE
Flatbush Dutch Reformed Church *S.W. cor. Flatbush and Church aves.*	Thomas Fardon	1793–96	Georgian	C.H.O.
*Erasmus Hall Academy (Erasmus Hall High School) *Flatbush Ave. near Church Ave.*	Attributed to Major L'Enfant	1787	Federal	H.
*Lefferts Homestead (D.A.R. Headquarters) *Prospect Park near Flatbush Ave.*	Unknown	1776	Dutch Colonial	H.O.
*Litchfield Mansion *Prospect Park near Prospect Park West and 5th St.*	Alexander J. Davis	1855–56	Modified Italianate	C.I.O.
Pieter Claesen Wyckoff house *Canarsie Lane Junction of Clarendon Road and Ralph Ave.*	Unknown	c.1640	Dutch Colonial	H.

CATEGORY II. Structures of great local or regional importance which should be preserved

STRUCTURE	ARCHITECT	DATE	STYLE	CODE
*Flatlands (Dutch Reformed) Church *Kings Highway and East 40th St.*	Unknown (Henry Eldert, builder)	1848	Greek Revival	H.
Holy Trinity Church *N.W. cor. Montague and Clinton sts.*	Minard Lafever	1844–47	Gothic Revival	C.G.O.
*Borough Hall *Fulton and Court sts.*	Gamaliel King	1846–48	Greek Revival	C.H.
Cupola added	C. W. and A. A. Stroughton	1898	Classic Eclectic	
Commandant's House New York Navy Yard *West side of enclosure*	Attributed to Charles Bulfinch	1805–06	Federal	H.
Hospital Building inside New York Navy Yard *263 Flushing Ave.*	Martin E. Thompson	1830–38	Modified Greek Revival	H.
Alexander M. White residence (Mrs. Darwin James, III) *2 Pierrepont Place*	Frederic A. Peterson	1856–57	Italianate	C.
Abiel A. Low residence (Mrs. Stephen Loines) *3 Pierrepont Place*	Frederic A. Peterson	1856–57	Italianate	C.
Eugene Boisselet residence *S.E. cor. Middagh and Willow sts.*	Unknown	c.1825	Federal	C.
*Schenck-Wyckoff house *1325 Flushing Ave.*	Unknown			
West end		c.1720	Dutch Colonial	
East end		1788		
Hitchcock, Pomeroy, and Brinkerhoff houses *155–157–159 Willow St. near Pierrepont St.*	Unknown	c.1825	Federal	C.
Brooklyn Savings Bank *N.E. cor. Clinton and Pierrepont sts.*	Frank Freeman	1893	Classic Eclectic	O.P.S.

CATEGORY III. Structures of importance designated for preservation

Churches

STRUCTURE	ARCHITECT	DATE	STYLE	CODE
Church of the Pilgrims (now Our Lady of Lebanon) *N.E. cor. Remsen and Henry sts.*	Richard Upjohn	1844–45	Romanesque Revival (Early)	C.H.
Friends' Meeting House *110 Schermerhorn St.*	Enoch Straton, builder	c.1854	Late Vernacular Greek Revival	
Grace (P.E.) Church *S.W. cor. Hicks St. and Grace Court*	Richard Upjohn	1847–48	Gothic Revival	O.S.
New Lots Dutch Reformed Church *New Lots and Schenck aves.*	Unknown	1823–24	Georgian-Gothic	C.
Plymouth Church of the Pilgrims (Beecher's church) *Orange St. near Hicks St.*	J. C. Wells	1849	Italianate	H.
St. Ann's (P.E.) Church *N.E. cor. Clinton and Livingston sts.*	Renwick and Sands	1867–69	Victorian Gothic	O.
St. Barbara's Church *S.W. cor. Bleecker St. and Central Ave.*	Helmle and Huberty	1893	Italian Renaissance Eclectic	O.

Public Buildings and Monuments

STRUCTURE	ARCHITECT	DATE	STYLE	CODE
Brooklyn Fire Headquarters (old) *365–367 Jay St.*	Frank Freeman	1891–92	Romanesque Revival	O.
Brooklyn Polytechnic Institute *N.E. cor. Court and Livingston sts.*	Frederic A. Peterson	1855	Italianate	
Addition	W. B. Tubby	1890	Romanesque Revival	O.
Grand Army Plaza *Eastern Parkway and Flatbush Ave.*	Olmsted, Vaux & Co.	1866		
Soldiers and Sailors Memorial Arch	John H. Duncan	1889–92	Roman Eclectic	C.L.S.

STRUCTURE	ARCHITECT	DATE	STYLE	CODE
Grand Army Plaza				
Sculpture on Arch (Quadriga)	Frederick MacMonnies			s.
Entrance to Prospect Park at Ocean Ave.	Stanford White	1894	Classic Eclectic	c.l.
"The Horse Tamers"	Frederick MacMonnies	1890	Classic Eclectic	s.
*Green-Wood Cemetery Gates *Fifth Ave. at 25th St.*	Richard Upjohn and Son	1861	Gothic Revival	c.o.s.
Main Post Office *Johnson St. between Washington and Adams sts.*	Mifflin E. Bell (Supervising Architect U.S. Treasury Department)	1885–91	Romanesque Revival	o.
Extended	James A. Wetmore (do.)	1933		
Municipal Building *Fulton and Joralemon sts.*	McKenzie, Voorhees, Gmelin and Walker	1924	Modified Roman Eclectic	o.
*Packer Collegiate Institute *170 Joralemon St.*	Minard Lafever	1854	Gothic Revival	c.g.

Commercial Buildings

STRUCTURE	ARCHITECT	DATE	STYLE	CODE
Franklin Trust Company *S.W. cor. Montague and Clinton sts.*	George L. Morse	1888	Romanesque Revival	o.
*Kings County Savings Bank *N.E. cor. Broadway and Bedford Ave.*	King and Wilcox	1868	French influence (Second Empire)	
*Williamsburg Savings Bank *N.W. cor. Broadway and Driggs Ave.*	George B. Post	1875	Classic Revival	c.o.
Remodeled		1905, 1923, 1942		

Clubs and Houses

STRUCTURE	ARCHITECT	DATE	STYLE	CODE
Hendrick I. Lott house (east wing) *1940 East 36th St.*	Unknown	c.1720	Dutch Colonial	h.
Enlarged		1800		
*Montauk Club *N.E. cor. Lincoln Place and Eighth Ave.*	Francis H. Kimball	1891	Venetian Gothic Eclectic	c.o.

STRUCTURE	ARCHITECT	DATE	STYLE	CODE
Van Nuyse-Magaw house *1041 East 22nd St.*	Unknown	c.1800–03	Dutch Colonial	H.
Wyckoff-Bennett house *1662 East 22nd St.*	Unknown	c.1766	Dutch Colonial	H.

CATEGORY "F." Structures of note filed for ready reference

STRUCTURE	ARCHITECT	DATE	STYLE	CODE
Christ (P.E.) Church *S.W. cor. Clinton and* *Kane sts.*	Richard Upjohn	1841	Gothic Revival	G.O.
*First Unitarian Church (formerly Church of the Saviour) *N.E. cor. Pierrepont St.* *and Monroe Place*	Minard Lafever	1844	Gothic Revival	O.
New Utrecht Reformed Church *S.W. cor. Eighteenth Ave.* *and 83rd St.,* *New Utrecht*	Unknown	1828	Georgian-Gothic	C.H.
South Bushwick Reformed Church *N.E. cor. Bushwick Ave.* *and Himrod St.*	Unknown	1851	Greek Revival (late)	H.
Hotel Margaret *N.E. cor. Columbia* *Heights and Orange St.*	Frank Freeman	1889	Romanesque Revival	I.O.
Van Sicklen house (Lady Moody house) *27 Gravesend Neck Road*	Unknown	c.1659	Dutch Colonial	H.
*Emmanuel Baptist Church *N.W. cor. Lafayette Ave.* *and Saint James Pl.*	Francis H. Kimball	1885–87	French Gothic Eclectic	O.
Charles Millard Pratt residence (now residence of Bishop of the Diocese of Brooklyn) *241 Clinton Ave.*	W. B. Tubby	1893	Romanesque Revival	O.

STRUCTURE	ARCHITECT	DATE	STYLE	CODE
*Henry C. Hulbert residence (now Brooklyn Society for Ethical Culture) *S.W. cor. Prospect Park West and 1st St.*	Montrose W. Morris	1881–83	Romanesque Revival	
Ami Dows residence *107 State St.*	Unknown	c.1846	Gothic Revival	I.
C. W. Rockwell residence *126 Willow St.*	Unknown	c.1830	Federal	O.
Cady, Rumrill, Peckam and Hathaway residences *20, 22, 24, 26 Willow St.* (22, Henry Ward Beecher, *1848*)	Unknown	c.1846	Greek Revival (row houses)	C.I.O.
John Dimon residence *57 Livingston St.*	Unknown	c.1848	Greek Revival	I.
Mott Bedell residence *11 Cranberry St.*	Unknown	c.1836	Greek Revival	I.
Colonnaded row houses *43–49 Willow Place*	Unknown	c.1846	Greek Revival	C.
Row houses *2–8 Willow Place*	Unknown	c.1848	Gothic Revival	C.O.
Robert White residence *57 Willow St.*	Unknown	c.1825	Vernacular Federal	
Adrian Van Sinderen residence *70 Willow St.*	Unknown	c.1839	Greek Revival	I.
Henry C. Bowen residence *131 Hicks St.* (135 similar but altered)	Unknown	c.1848	Gothic Revival	I.O.
George Hastings residence *36 Pierrepont St.*	Unknown	c.1844	Gothic Revival	I.O.
Matilda Brown residence *52 Livingston St.*	Unknown	c.1847	Modified Gothic Revival	I.O.
Allen Lippincott residence *135 Joralemon St.*	Unknown	c.1830	Modified Federal	I.O.
Cast-iron porch added		c.1850		

BOROUGH OF BRONX

Buildings in Bronx Built Before 1930

CATEGORY I. Structures of national importance which should be preserved at all costs

STRUCTURE	ARCHITECT	DATE	STYLE	CODE
Bartow Mansion Museum (Headquarters of International Garden Club) *Shore Road, Pelham Bay Park*	Attributed to Minard Lafever	1836–42	Greek Revival	C.H.L. O.S.

CATEGORY II. Structures of great local or regional importance which should be preserved

*St. Ann's Church (Morris Tombs) *St. Ann's Ave. and 140th St.*	Unknown	1841	Gothic Revival	H.
Fort Schuyler *Throgg's Neck*	Designed by Captain I. L. Smith	1834–38	Military	C.H.
Restored		1934–38		
*Poe Cottage *Kingsbridge Road*	John Wheeler, builder	c.1812	Vernacular	C.H.
Van Cortlandt Manor *Van Cortlandt Park*	Unknown	1748	Georgian	H.
Bronx Zoo Central Buildings	Heins and LaFarge	c.1899	Modified Classic Eclectic	C.L.

CATEGORY III. Structures of Importance Designated for Protection

STRUCTURE	ARCHITECT	DATE	STYLE	CODE
*Christ Church *Riverdale Ave. and* *254th St.*	Richard M. Upjohn	1865–66	Gothic Revival	o.
Rectory		1872		
St. James Church *Jerome Ave. and 190th St.,* *Fordham*	Unknown	1864	Gothic Revival	o.
St. Peter's (R.C.) Church *2500 Westchester Ave.*	Leopold Eidlitz	1851–53	Gothic Revival	o.
Additions and alterations		1877, 1898, 1953		
Lorillard Snuff Mill *Botanical Garden* *Bronx Park*	Unknown	1840	Vernacular	c.h.
Remodeled		1953–54		
Hall of Fame New York University *181st St. and University* *Ave.*	McKim, Mead & White	1896–1900	Modified Roman Eclectic	c.h.
Mott Haven Railroad Station clock tower *138th St. near Harlem R.*	R. H. Robertson	1886	Romanesque Revival	c.o.

CATEGORY "F." Structures of note filed for ready reference

STRUCTURE	ARCHITECT	DATE	STYLE	CODE
Riverdale Presbyterian Church *Henry Hudson Parkway* *Riverdale*	Attributed to James Renwick, Jr.	1863	Gothic Revival	c.
"Wave Hill" *645 West 252nd St.* *Riverdale*	Unknown	c.1830	Late Federal	h.l.
South wing	Oliver P. Morton of Putnam and Cox	1931		

BOROUGH OF QUEENS

Buildings in Queens Built Before 1930

CATEGORY I. Structures of national importance which should be preserved at all costs

STRUCTURE	ARCHITECT	DATE	STYLE	CODE
Bowne House *Bowne St. and Fox Lane* *Flushing*	John J. Bowne, builder	1661	Early American	C.H.
*Old Quaker Meeting House *Northern Boulevard* *Flushing*	Unknown	1695	Early American	C.H.

CATEGORY II. Structures of great local and regional importance which should be preserved

STRUCTURE	ARCHITECT	DATE	STYLE	CODE
Bodine Castle *43–16 Vernon Boulevard* *Long Island City*	Unknown	1840	Modified Gothic Revival	C.
*Lent Homestead *7805 Nineteenth Road* *Steinway*	Unknown	17th century	Dutch Colonial	C.H.
Rufus King Mansion *Jamaica Ave. and 153rd St.* *Jamaica*	Unknown	1755	Georgian	C.H.

CATEGORY III. Structures of importance designated for preservation

STRUCTURE	ARCHITECT	DATE	STYLE	CODE
Grand Avenue house *8604 Grand Ave.* *Elmhurst*	Unknown	c.1840	Greek Revival	C.
Kingsland homestead *46–25 155th St.* *Flushing*	Unknown	1774–85	Early American	C.H.
*St. George's (Episcopal) Church *135–32 38th Ave.* *Flushing*	Wills and Dudley	1848–52	Gothic Revival	O.
Twenty-Seventh Avenue house *417 27th Ave.* *Astoria*	David Paten	c.1840	Greek Revival	C.

CATEGORY "F." Structures of note filed for ready reference

STRUCTURE	ARCHITECT	DATE	STYLE	CODE
Fourth Street house *26–35 4th St.* *Astoria*	Unknown	c.1840	Greek Revival	
Twelfth Street house *26–07 12th St.* *Astoria*	Unknown	c.1840	Greek Revival	

BOROUGH OF RICHMOND (STATEN ISLAND)

Buildings in Richmond Built Before 1930

CATEGORY I. Structures of national importance which should be preserved at all costs

STRUCTURE	ARCHITECT	DATE	STYLE	CODE
*Billopp (Conference) House *Hylan Boulevard and Satterlee St., Tottenville*	Christopher Billopp, owner-builder	c.1695	Dutch Colonial	C.H.
Sailors' Snug Harbor *Richmond Terrace New Brighton*	Martin E. Thompson	1831–33	Greek Revival	C.H.L.

CATEGORY II. Structures of great local or regional importance which should be preserved

Austen house *2 Hylan Boulevard Rosebank*	Unknown	c.1680	Early American	C.H.
Addition on Narrows	Attributed to James Renwick, Jr.	c.1850	Gothic Revival	O.
Billiou-Stillwell-Perine house *1467 Richmond Road Dongan Hills*	Unknown	1662	Early American	C.H.
Additions		1750, 1790, 1830		C.H.

STRUCTURE	ARCHITECT	DATE	STYLE	CODE
Christopher house *Willowbrook Road*	Unknown	c.1767	Early American	C.H.
*Dutch Reformed Church *Richmond Ave. opposite Church St. Port Richmond*	Unknown	1845	Modified Greek Revival	G.
Lake-Tysen house *Richmondtown*	Daniel Lake, owner-architect	c.1740	Dutch Colonial	C.
"Old Stone Jug" Neville house *806 Richmond Terrace New Brighton*	Unknown	1770	Early American	C.
*Original Moravian Church *Richmond Road, New Dorp*	Unknown	c.1763	Dutch Colonial	C.H.
United States Marine Hospital *Bay St. and Vanderbilt Ave. Stapleton*	George B. Davis, builder	1837	Greek Revival	C.H.L.
Voorlezer's house *Arthur Kill Road opposite Centre St. Richmondtown*	Unknown	c.1695	Dutch Colonial	C.H.
Restored		1940		

CATEGORY III. Structures of importance designated for protection

St. Andrew's Episcopal Church *Richmond Hill and Old Mill Rd. Richmondtown*	William Mersereau	1872	Gothic Revival	C.G.H.
Britton-Cubberly cottage *New Dorp Lane New Dorp*	Unknown	c.1677	Early American	H.
Cortelyou house *Richmond Road New Dorp*	Unknown	c.1676	Early American	C.H.
Columbia Hall *404 Richmond Terrace New Brighton*	Unknown	c.1835	Greek Revival	C.

STRUCTURE	ARCHITECT	DATE	STYLE	CODE
Holmes-Cole house *Hylan Boulevard* *Great Kills*	Unknown	c.1720	Dutch Colonial	C.H.
Restored		1940		
Houseman house *308 St. John's Ave.* *Westerleigh*	Unknown	c.1750	Early American	C.
Kruser-Pelton house *1262 Richmond Terrace* *West New Brighton*	Unknown	1722	Early American	C.
Central section added		1770		
Purdy's Hotel *509 Seguine Ave.* *Prince's Bay*	Unknown	c.1690	Early American	C.H.
Scott-Edwards house *752 Delafield Ave.* *West New Brighton*	Unknown	c.1750	Early American	C.
Third County Courthouse *Center St.* *Richmondtown*	Unknown	1837	Greek Revival	C.H.

CATEGORY "F." Structures of note filed for ready reference

Biddle Mansion *70 Satterlee St.* *Tottenville*	Unknown	c.1840	Greek Revival	C.
*St. John's Episcopal Church *Bay St., Rosebank*	Arthur Gilman	1869	Gothic Revival	C.
St. Mary's Episcopal Church *Castleton Ave.* *West New Brighton*	Unknown	1858	Gothic Revival	C.
*St. Paul's Episcopal Church *St. Paul's Ave.* *Tompkinsville*	Unknown	1866–70	Gothic Revival	C.G.
Woodrow Methodist Episcopal Church *Woodrow Road, Woodrow*	Unknown	c.1842	Greek Revival	C.H.

IX. BIBLIOGRAPHY

Compiled by the Editor

INTRODUCTION

VIOLLET-LE-DUC once said that to know the past helps us to understand the future better. In the realm of architecture, understanding can best be achieved through a study of the buildings themselves. This study can be supplemented and interpreted through books written about the architecture we seek. The following bibliography may be considered a reading list. The books are grouped under various subjects to help and encourage the reader in his quest.

NOTE: Entries in this bibliography are arranged alphabetically by author except in the section "Architects," where the arrangement is alphabetical by subject.

HISTORIES — GENERAL

Manhattan

Abbott, Berenice, and McCausland, Elizabeth, *Changing New York*. E. P. Dutton & Co., Inc., 1939.

Albion, Robert G., *The Rise of the New York Port, 1815–1860*. Charles Scribner's Sons, 1939.

Belden, E. Porter, *New York; Past, Present and Future*. . . . G. P. Putnam, 1849.

Bonner, William T., *New York: The World's Metropolis, 1624–1924*. . . . R. L. Polk & Co., 1924. (Bibliography.)

Booth, Mary L., *History of the City of New York From Its Earliest Settlement* . . . (2 vols.). Clark & Meeker, 1867.

Brown, Henry Collins, *Valentine's Manual of the City of New York* (New Series). Valentine's Manual, Inc., 1916–1927.

————, *In the Golden Nineties*. Valentine's Manual, Inc., 1928.

————, *Old New York, Yesterday and Today*. Privately printed for Valentine's Manual, 1922.

Brown, Thomas Allston, *The History of the New York Stage* (3 vols.). Dodd, Mead & Co., 1903.

Browne, Junius Henri, *The Great Metropolis; A Mirror of New York.* . . . American Publishing Co., 1869.

Burnham, Alan, "Architecture of New York City — A Personal Bookshelf." *Art in America* Vol. 45, No. 2, Summer, 1957.

Chambers, Julius, *The Book of New York: Forty Years Recollections.* . . . Book of New York Co., 1912.

Clary, Martin, *Mid-Manhattan — The Multimillionarea.* Forty-second Street Property Owners' and Merchants' Association, Inc., 1929.

Colton, Julia M., *Annals of Old Manhattan, 1609–1664.* Brentano's, 1901.

Despard, Matilda Pratt, *Old New York from the Battery to Bloomingdale.* G. P. Putnam's Sons, 1875.

De Voe, Thomas, *The Market Book — A History of the Public Markets in the City of New York from its First Settlements to the Present Time.* Printed for the author, 1862.

Dilliard, Maud Esther, *An Album of New Netherland.* Twayne Publishers, Inc., 1963. (Bibliography.)

Dunlap, William, *History of the New Netherlands* . . . *1609–1789* (2 vols.). Carter & Thorp, 1839.

Dunshee, Kenneth Holcomb, *As You Pass By.* Hastings House, 1952.

Earle, Alice Morse, *Colonial Days in Old New York.* Charles Scribner's Sons, 1896.

Fay, Theodore S., *Views of New York and Its Environs.* . . . Peabody & Co., 1831.

Francis, John W., *Old New York or Reminiscences of the Past Sixty Years.* W. J. Widdleton, 1865.

Goodwin, Royce, and Putnam, editors. *Historic New York — Half Moon Papers* (2 vols.). Knickerbocker Press, 1898.

Hardy, John, *Manual of the Corporation of the City of New York — 1870.*

Harrison, Mrs. Burton, "Externals of Modern New York" (Chapter XXI, Martha Lamb, *History of the City of New York,* Vol. II). A. S. Barnes & Co., 1896.

Hemstreet, Charles, *The Story of Manhattan.* Charles Scribner's Sons, 1901.

————, *When Old New York Was Young.* Charles Scribner's Sons, 1902.

Janvier, Thomas A., *The Dutch Founding of New York.* Harper & Brothers, 1903.

————, *In Old New York.* Harper & Brothers, 1894.

Kelley, Frank Bergen, compiler, *Historical Guide to the City of New York.* Frederick A. Stokes Co., 1909. (Bibliographies.)

King, Moses, editor. *King's Handbook of New York City.* Moses King, 1892 (1893).

————, *King's Views of New York — 1908–1909.* Moses King, 1908.

————, *King's Photographic Views of New York.* . . . Moses King, 1895.

Kouwenhoven, John A., *The Columbia Historical Portrait of New York.* Doubleday & Company, Inc., 1953.

Lamb, Martha J., *History of the City of New York* . . . (2 vols.). A. S. Barnes & Co., 1877.

Leonard, John W., *History of the City of New York 1609–1909* (2 vols.). *New York Journal of Commerce and Commercial Bulletin,* 1910.

Little Old New York Illustrated. Oxford Publishing Company, 1910.

Look, editors of, in collaboration with Frederick Lewis Allen, *Look at America: New York City* (regional volume). Houghton Mifflin Company, 1948.

Lossing, Benson J., *History of New York City 1609–1884* (2 vols.). Perine Engraving & Publishing Co., 1884.

McCabe, James D., *Lights and Shadows of New York Life.* . . . National Publishing Co., 1872.

————, *New York by Sunlight and Gaslight.* . . . Union Publishing House, 1882.

McGinnis, Edith, *Know Your City — A School Broadcast Manual for Teachers and Parents.* City History Club of New York, 1954. (Bibliography.)

Mayer, Grace, *Once Upon A City*. The Macmillan Company, 1958.

Moss, Frank, *The American Metropolis* . . . (3 vols.). Peter Fenelon Collier Press, 1897.

New York City Guide: A Comprehensive Guide to the Five Boroughs of the Metropolis . . . (American Guide Series, W.P.A.). Random House, 1939. (Historic houses indexed; bibliography.)

New York City Guide and Almanac 1961–62. New York University Press, 1962. (Bibliography pp. 109–112.)

New-York Historical Society Quarterly and other publications. (For a complete list of titles, consult R. R. Bowker's *Publications of Societies*.)

New York Panorama (American Guide Series, W.P.A.). Random House, 1938.

New York the Metropolis. . . . The New York Recorder, 1893.

Odell, George C. D., *Annals of the New York Stage* (15 vols.). Columbia University Press, 1927–1945.

Pasko, W. W., editor, *Old New York: A Journal Relating to the History and Antiquities of New York City* (2 vols.). W. W. Pasko, 1890.

Pelletreau, William S., *Historic Homes and Institutions and Genealogical and Family History of New York* (4 vols.). Lewis Publishing Co., 1907.

Peterson, A. Everett, *Landmarks of New York — An Historical Guide to the Metropolis*. City History Club of New York, 1923.

Picture of New York in 1846 with a Short Account of Places in Its Vicinity. Homans & Ellis, 1846.

Reed, Henry Hope, Jr., *Walks in New York. . . .* Clarkson N. Potter, 1963.

Reynolds, James B., editor, *Civic Bibliography for Greater New York*. New York Research Council, Charities Publication Committee, 1911. (Bibliography 296 pages.)

Richmond, J. F., *New York and Its Institutions 1609–1873 — The Bright Side of New York*. E. B. Treat, 1871 (1873).

Rider's New York City . . . The Macmillan Company, 1924. (Bibliography p. 128.)

Riverside — A Study of Housing on the West Side of New York. By The Committee on Housing, New York Chapter, American Institute of Architects, Henry S. Churchill, Chairman. Sponsored by the Fred L. Lavanburg Foundation, 1954.

Shackleton, Robert, *The Book of New York*. The Penn Publishing Co., 1917.

Shannon, Joseph, *Manual of the Corporation of the City of New York* (2 vols.). 1868 and 1869.

Smith, Matthew Hale, *Sunshine and Shadow in New York*. J. B. Burr & Co., 1868.

Stokes, Isaac Newton Phelps, *Iconography of Manhattan Island* (6 vols.). Robert H. Dodd, 1915–1928. (Bibliography.)

Stone, William L., *History of New York City. . . .* Virtue & Yorston, 1872.

The Sun, editors of, *New York in Pictures* (2 vols.). Reprinted from *The Sun*, 1928.

The Sun, editors of, *Facts About New York*. Reprinted from *The Sun*, 1927.

Todd, Charles Burr, *Story of the City of New York*. G. P. Putnam's Sons, 1902.

Ulmann, Albert, *A Landmark History of New York*. D. Appleton & Co., 1914. (Bibliography pp. 267–279.)

Valentine, David T., *History of the City of New York*. G. P. Putnam & Co., 1853.

———, *Manual of the Common Council of New York* (26 vols.). *Valentine's Manuals* various publishers, 1842–1867.

Van Pelt, Daniel, *Leslie's History of the Greater New York* (3 vols.). Arkell Publishing Co., 1898.

Van Rensselaer, Mrs. Schuyler, *History of the City of New York in the Seventeenth Century* (2 vols.). The Macmillan Company, 1909.

Wilson, James Grant, *Memorial History of the City of New-York* (3 vols.). New York History Co., 1892.

Wilson, Rufus Rockwell, *New York Old and New; Its Story, Streets and Landmarks* (2 vols.). J. B. Lippincott Co., 1903.

Wood's Illustrated Handbook to New York and Environs . . . G. W. Carleton & Co., 1873.

Zeisloft, E. Idell, *The New Metropolis, 1600–1900.* D. Appleton & Co., 1899.

BLOOMINGDALE

Mott, Hopper Striker, *The New York of Yesterday — A Descriptive Narrative of Old Bloomingdale.* . . . G. P. Putnam's Sons, 1908.

BOWERY

Harlow, Alvin F., *Old Bowery Days.* D. Appleton & Co., 1931.

CHELSEA

Chelsea Corners Tatler, Vol. 1, No. 1, 1931.

Patterson, Samuel White, *Old Chelsea and Saint Peter's Church.* The Friebele Press, 1935.

GREENWICH VILLAGE

Arens, Egmont, *The Little Book About Greenwich Village.* E. Arens, 1918.

Bartholomew, Ralph I., *Greenwich Village.* Publishers Printing Company, 1920.

Chapin, Anna Alice, *Greenwich Village.* Dodd, Mead & Co., 1917.

Henderson, Helen W., *A Loiterer in New York* . . . (esp. Chapter IX, "Greenwich Village — The Bossen Bouwerie"). George H. Doran Co., 1917.

Lanier, Henry Wysham, and Abbott, Berenice (photos), *Greenwich Village Today and Yesterday.* Harper & Brothers, 1949.

Pierre, C. Grand, *The Little Book of Greenwich Village. The Greenwich Village Weekly News,* 1935.

———, *Rambling Through Greenwich Village. The Greenwich Village Weekly News,* 1935.

Simkhovitch, (Mrs.) Mary Melinda (Kingsbury), *Neighborhood: My Story of Greenwich Village.* W. W. Norton & Company, Inc., 1938.

Ware, Caroline F., *Greenwich Village 1920–1930 — A Comment on American Civilization in the Post-War Years.* Houghton Mifflin Company, 1935.

HARLEM

Levick, M. B., "Last of Harlem's Country Seats." *New York Times Magazine*, April 15, 1923.

Pierce, Carl Horton, *New Harlem, Past and Present.* . . . New Harlem Publishing Co., 1903.

Riker, James, *Harlem, Its Origin and Early Annals.* . . . James Riker, 1881.

Van Pelt, Daniel, *Leslie's History of the Greater New York*, Vol. I, (esp. Chapter XVI, "The City Crosses the Harlem River"). Arkell Publishing Co., 1898.

Bronx

Bolton, Robert, *The History of the Several Towns, Manors and Patents of the County of Westchester* (2 vols.). Charles F. Roper, 1881 (1905).

Comfort, Randall, *History of Bronx Borough.* North Side News Press, 1906.

Comstock, Sarah, *Old Roads from the Heart of New York Within Thirty Miles Around the Battery.* G. P. Putnam's Sons, 1915.

Cook, Harry T., and Kaplan, Nathan J. *The Borough of the Bronx, 1639–1913.* . . . Published by the authors, 1913.

Cushman, Elisabeth, *Historic Westchester, 1683–1933 — Glimpses of a County History.* Westchester County Publishing Co., 1933.

Fitzpatrick, Benedict, *The Bronx and Its People*. The Lewis Historical Publishing Co., 1927.

Hansen, Harry, *North of Manhattan — Persons and Places of Old Westchester.* Hastings House, 1950.

Jenkins, Stephen, *The Greatest Street in the World . . .* (Broadway). G. P. Putnam's Sons, 1911.

————, *The Story of the Bronx . . . 1639 to the Present Day.* G. P. Putnam's Sons, 1912.

Kelley, Frank B., *Historical Guide to the City of New York. . . .* City History Club, 1913.

Melick, Harry C., *The Manor of Fordham and Its Founder.* Fordham University Press, 1950.

Pelletreau, William S., *Historic Homes and Institutions and Genealogical and Family History of New York.* Lewis Publishing Co., 1907.

Scharf, J. Thomas, *History of Westchester County Including Morrisania, Kingsbridge and West Farms* (2 vols.). L. E. Preston, 1886.

Schliessman, Ronald (compiler), *The Bronx in the World of Books.* Bronx County Historical Society, 1960.

Shonnard, Frederic, and Spooner, W. W., *History of Westchester County From Its Earliest Settlement to the Year 1900.* New York History Co., 1900.

Tieck, William A., *God's House and the Old Kingsbridge Road.* Christensen & Boesen, Inc., Printers, 1948.

Van Pelt, Daniel, *Leslie's History of the Greater New York,* Vol. II (esp. Chapter XXII, "The Bronx"). Arkell Publishing Co., 1898.

Wells, James, et al., editors. *The Bronx and Its People — A History 1609–1927* (4 vols.). The Lewis Historical Publishing Co., 1927.

NOTE: Consult also publications of The Bronx County Historical Society, 90–B Edgewater Park, Bronx 65, New York City.

Brooklyn

Armbruster, Eugene L., *Brooklyn's Eastern District.* (No publisher given), 1942.

Brooklyn's Garden — Views of Picturesque Flatbush. Charles Andrew Ditmas, 1908.

Brooklyn Savings Bank, *Old Brooklyn Heights, 1827–1927.* John G. Powers Co., Inc., 1927.

Brooklyn Trust Company, *Rambles About Historic Brooklyn. . . .* Walton Advertising and Printing Co., 1916.

Burnham, Alan, "Forgotten Engineering — Post and Lintel Postdated" (the story of Niels Poulson, proprietor of the Hecla Iron Works). *The Architectural Record,* Vol. 127, No. 5, May 1960.

Callender, James H., *Yesterdays on Brooklyn Heights.* The Dorland Press, 1927.

Cleaveland, Nehemiah, *Greenwood [Cemetery] Illustrated in a Series of Views Taken Expressly for this Work by James Smillie.* R. Martin, 1847.

————, *Hints Concerning Greenwood [Cemetery], Its Monuments and Improvements.* Pudney & Russell, 1853.

Dilliard, Maud E., *Old Dutch Houses of Brooklyn.* Richard R. Smith, 1945.

Ditmas, Charles A., *Historic Homesteads of King's County* (limited ed'n.). 1909.

Field, Thomas W., *Historic and Antiquarian Scenes in Brooklyn and Its Vicinity. . . .* (No publisher given), 1868.

Fisher, Edmund D., *Flatbush Past and Present.* Flatbush Trust Co., 1901.

Glimpses of Brooklyn. Mercantile Illustrating Co., 1894.

Hazelton, Henry I., *History of Brooklyn and Long Island.* Pearl Press, 1923.

Howard, Henry W. B., editor, *The Eagle and Brooklyn. . . . Brooklyn Daily Eagle,* 1893.

Huntington, Edna, *Historical Markers and Monuments in Brooklyn.* Long Island Historical Society, 1952.

King, Moses, editor, *King's Views of Brooklyn.* Moses King, 1904.

Lancaster, Clay, *New York's First Suburb Old Brooklyn Heights Including Detailed Analyses of 619 Century-Old Houses.* Charles E. Tuttle Co., Inc., 1961.

Langstaff, B. Meredith, *Brooklyn Heights Yesterday, Today, Tomorrow.* Published under the auspices of the Brooklyn Heights Association, 1937.

Long Island Historical Society Quarterly, Vol. 1, No. 1, 1939. (Contains many valuable articles on Brooklyn history and architecture.)

Mead, D. Irving, *Historical Sketch of the South Brooklyn Savings Institution.* Boice Du Bois, 1924.

Ostrander, Stephen M., *History of the City of Brooklyn and Kings County.* Published by subscription, 1894.

Poole, Ernest, *The Harbor.* The Macmillan Company, 1915 (1942).

Reed, Henry Hope, Jr., and Bayley, John Barrington, *Classical Brooklyn: Its Architecture and Sculpture.* Under the sponsorship of the Long Island Historical Society and the Municipal Art Society, 1956. (Mimeographed catalogue for an exhibition at the Long Island Historical Society.)

Riverside Buildings of the Improved Dwellings Company. Evening Post Job Printery, 1890. (See also earlier editions.)

Souvenir of Brooklyn: Descriptive, Historical and Statistical Review. Walbridge & Co., 1890.

Stiles, Henry R., *A History of the City of Brooklyn . . .* (3 vols.). Published by subscription, 1867–1870.

———, editor-in-chief, *History of King's County, 1683–1884* (2 vols.). W. W. Munsell & Co., 1884.

Strong, Thomas M., *History of the Town of Flatbush in Kings County.* Thomas R. Mercen, 1842.

Vanderbilt, Gertrude Lefferts, *Social History of Flatbush.* D. Appleton & Co., 1881.

Van Pelt, Daniel, *Leslie's History of the Greater New York,* Vol. II (esp. Chapters VI through XV). Arkell Publishing Co., 1898.

Views of Brooklyn. L. H. Nelson Co., 1905.

Weld, Ralph, *Brooklyn Village.* Columbia University Press, 1938.

Witteman, A., *Brooklyn.* Albertype Co., 1904.

Wilson, James Grant, *Memorial History of the City of New-York . . .* (esp. Vol. IV, Chapter I, "The City of Brooklyn," by Henry R. Stiles). New York History Co., 1892.

NOTE: Consult also: publications and indexed scrapbooks of The Long Island Historical Society, Pierrepont and Clinton Sts., Brooklyn, N.Y., photo collection of Brooklyn Public Library, and the following publications: *Holiday,* June 1950, February 1959, March 1960; *Journal of Long Island History,* Vol. 1, No. 1, 1961; *Long Island Forum,* Vol. 1, No. 1, January 1938 (index 1938–1947 and 1948–1952).

Queens

Frost, Josephine C., editor, *Records of the Town of Jamaica, Long Island, 1656–1751* (3 vols.). Long Island Historical Society, 1914.

Hall, Courtney R., "Some Impressions of Flushing." *The Journal of Long Island History,* Vol. 1, No. 1, Spring 1961.

Mandeville, G. Henry, *Flushing Past and Present.* J. Egbert, Printer, 1860.

Onderdonk, Henry, Jr., *Revolutionary Incidents of Queens County.* Henry Leavitt, Irow & Co., 1846.

Powell, Charles U., *The Quakers in Flushing 1657–1937.* Case, Printers, 1937.

Riker, James, Jr., *Annals of Newtown, in Queens County, New York. . . .* D. Fanshaw, 1852.

Trebor, Haynes, *Colonial Flushing.* Flushing Federal Savings & Loan Association, 1945.

————, *Bowne House — A Shrine to Religious Freedom*. Flushing Savings Bank, 1947.

Valles, Madeline B., *History of Flushing*. Master's thesis, unpublished, Columbia, 1938.

Van Pelt, Daniel, *Leslie's History of the Greater New York*, Vol. II (esp. Chapters XVI through XIX). Arkell Publishing Co., 1898.

Waller, Henry D., *History of the Town of Flushing*. J. H. Ridenour, 1899.

Willis, Walter I., editor, *Queens Borough, 1910–1920*. Chamber of Commerce of the Borough of Queens, 1920.

NOTE: Consult Historical Department, Queensborough Public Library, 89–14 Parsons Boulevard, Jamaica, N.Y.

Staten Island (Richmond)

Bayles, Richard M., *History of Richmond County, Staten Island, N.Y.* L. E. Preston & Co. 1887.

Clute, J. J., *The Annals of Staten Island*. Charles Vogt, 1877.

Gillespie, Harriet S., "Historic Dutch Houses Upon Staten Island." *Country Life in America*, Vol. 31, No. 6, April 1917.

Hine, Charles Gilbert, *History of the Perine House*. Staten Island Antiquarian Society, Inc., 1915.

Leng, Charles W., and Davis, William T., *Staten Island and Its People* (4 vols.). Lewis Historical Publishing Co., 1930.

Morris, I. K., *Memorial History of Staten Island* (2 vols.). Memorial Publishing Co., 1898–1900.

Picturesque Staten Island, The Gateway to New York Harbor. The Staten Island Amusement Co., 1886.

Richmondtown Restoration, Staten Island, New York. Department of Parks, Staten Island Historical Society, and Richmondtown Restoration, 1962.

Steinmeyer, Henry G., *Staten Island, 1524–1898*. Staten Island Historical Society, 1950.

Van Pelt, Daniel, *Leslie's History of the Greater New York*, Vol. II (esp. Chapter XX, "Richmond or Staten Island — Olden Times"; Chapter XXI, "Richmond or Staten Island — Present Century"). Arkell Publishing Co., 1898.

Wilson, James Grant, *Memorial History of the City of New-York . . .* , Vol. IV (esp. Chapter I, "Staten Island," by Walter S. Wilson). New York History Co., 1892.

NOTE: Consult Staten Island Historical Society, Richmondtown, Staten Island 6, N.Y.

ARCHITECTURE — GENERAL

Andrews, Wayne, *Architecture, Ambition and Americans*. Harper & Brothers, 1947. (Bibliography.)

Architectural League of New York, Catalogues and Yearbooks from 1886 onward. (Architecture and Sculpture — Annual Exhibitions.)

Bach, Richard Franz, "A Bibliography of the Literature of Colonial Architecture." *Architectural Record*, Vol. 38, No. 3, September 1915, to Vol. 44, No. 2, August 1918.

Badger, Daniel D., *Illustrations of Iron Architecture Made by the Architectural Iron Works of the City of New York*. Baker & Godwin, 1865.

Birkmire, William H., *The Planning and Construction of High Office-Buildings*. John Wiley & Sons, 1898.

Burchard, J., and Bush-Brown, A., *The Architecture of America — A Social and Cultural History*. Little, Brown & Co., 1961. (Bibliography and Index of Architects, p. 541.)

Chase, W. Parker, *New York The Wonder City. . . .* Wonder City Publishing Co., 1932.

Condit, Carl W., *American Building Art — The Nineteenth Century.* Oxford University Press, 1960. (Bibliography.)

Edgell, George H., *The American Architecture of Today.* Charles Scribner's Sons, 1928. (Bibliography.)

Ferriss, Hugh, *Metropolis of Tomorrow.* Ives Washburn, Inc., 1929.

Field, M., *City Architecture.* . . . D. Appleton & Co., 1854.

Grady, James A., "Bibliography of the Art Nouveau." *Journal of the Society of Architectural Historians,* Vol. 14, No. 2, May 1955.

Hamlin, Talbot F., *The American Spirit in Architecture* (The Pageant of America, Vol. 13). Yale University Press, 1926.

——, *Greek Revival Architecture in America* . . . (esp. Chapter 6, "The Classic Revival in New York"). Oxford University Press, 1944. (Bibliography.)

Hegemann, Werner (Ruth Nanda Anshen, editor), *City Planning — Housing.* Architectural Book Publishing Co., 1937.

Historic American Buildings Survey — Catalogue of Measured Drawings and Photographs . . . (New York City p. 270; Bronx p. 260; Brooklyn p. 260). National Park Service, Department of the Interior, 1941. (Supplement, January, 1959.)

History of Architecture and the Building Trades of Greater New York (2 vols.). The Union History Co., 1899.

History of Real Estate, Building and Architecture in New York During the Last Quarter of a Century. Record & Guide, 1898.

Hitchcock, Henry-Russell, *Architecture, Nineteenth and Twentieth Centuries* (The Pelican History of Art). Penguin Books, 1958.

Hoak, E. W., and Church, W. H., *Masterpieces of Architecture in the United States.* Charles Scribner's Sons, 1930.

Jackson, Huson, *A Guide to New York Architecture, 1650–1952.* Reinhold Publishing Corp., 1952.

Jordy, William H., and Coe, Ralph, editors, *American Architecture and Other Writings by Montgomery Schuyler* (2 vols.). Harvard University Press, 1961. (Bibliography.)

Kennion, John W., *The Architects' and Builders' Guide.* . . . Fitzpatrick & Hunter, 1868.

Koch, Robert, "The Mediaeval Castle Revival: New York Armories." *Journal of the Society of Architectural Historians,* Vol. 4, No. 3, October 1955.

Lamb, (Mrs.) Martha J., "Historic Houses and Landmarks." *The Magazine of American History,* Vol. 21, March 1889.

Mujica, Francisco, *History of the Skyscraper.* Archaeology and Architecture Press, 1929.

Mumford, Lewis, *Sticks and Stones — A Study of American Architecture and Civilization.* W. W. Norton & Company, Inc., 1924.

Myer, John Walden, "Gothic Revival in New York." *Bulletin of the Museum of the City of New York,* Vol. 3, No. 5, April 1940.

New York Illustrated. D. Appleton & Co., 1870. (Also 1881 and 1884.)

New York Sketch Book of Architecture, Vol. I through Vol. III. James R. Osgood & Co., 1874–1876.

Old Buildings of New York City. . . . Brentano's, 1907.

Pelletreau, William S., *Historic Homes and Institutions, 1840–1918.* Lewis Publishing Co., 1918.

Price, C. Matlack, "A Renaissance in Commercial Architecture — Some Recent Buildings in Up-Town New York." *Architectural Record,* Vol. 31, No. 5, May 1912.

Reed, Henry Hope, Jr., *The Golden City.* Doubleday & Company, Inc., 1959.

——, and Davidson, Marshall B., guest editors, "New York: Exploring the Classical Tradition." *Art in America,* Vol. 45, No. 2, Summer 1957.

Roos, Frank J., Jr., *Writings on Early American Architecture and an Annotated List of Books and Articles on Architecture Constructed Before 1860. . . .* The Ohio State University Press, 1943. (New York City p. 127.)

Schuyler, Montgomery, *American Architecture — Studies.* Harper & Brothers, 1892. (See also Jordy.)

————, (articles signed "M.S."), "Recent Building in New York." *The American Architect & Building News,* as follows: I. "Public Buildings," Vol. 9, No. 276, April 9, 1881. II. "Commercial Buildings," Vol. 9, No. 277, April 16, 1881.

————, "The Romanesque Revival in New York." *The Architectural Record,* Vol. 1, No. 1, July–September 1891.

————, "Some Recent Skyscrapers." *The Architectural Record,* Vol. 22, No. 3, September 1907.

Starrett, W. A., *Skyscrapers and the Men Who Build Them.* Charles Scribner's Sons, 1928.

Sturges, Walter Knight, "Cast Iron in New York." *Architectural Review,* Vol. 114, No. 682, October 1953.

Van Derpool, James Grote, *Avery Memorial Architectural Library* (Appendix I, Bicentennial History of Columbia University — The School of Architecture). Columbia University Press, 1954.

Van Pelt, Daniel, *Leslie's History of the Greater New York,* Vol. III (esp. "Architecture and Building in New York," by the late Benson J. Lossing, pp. 705–731). Arkell Publishing Co., 1898. (See also biographies of New York City architects.)

Webster, J. Carson, "The Skyscraper: Logical and Historical Considerations." *Journal of the Society of Architectural Historians,* Vol. 18, No. 4, December 1959.

Weisman, Winston, "Commercial Palaces of New York, 1854–75." *Art Bulletin,* Vol. 36, No. 4, December 1954.

————, "New York and the Problem of the First Skyscraper." *Journal of the Society of Architectural Historians,* Vol. 12, No. 1, March 1953.

Williamson, Jefferson, *The American Hotel — An Anecdotal History* (esp. Chapters I, II, and III). Alfred A. Knopf, Inc., 1930.

NOTE: Consult also the following periodicals: *American Architect & Building News; The Architectural Record; Architectural Forum* (formerly *The Brickbuilder*); *Gramercy Graphic; Journal of the Society of Architectural Historians; News From Home* (magazine of the Home Life Insurance Company); *Progressive Architecture.*

ARCHITECTS

"Barney & Chapman, The Works of Messrs.," by Montgomery Schuyler. *The Architectural Record,* Vol. 16, No. 3, September 1904.

"Bogardus Revisited," by Turpin Bannister. *Journal of the Society of Architectural Historians;* Part I, "The Iron Fronts," Vol. 15, No. 4, December 1956; Part II, "The Iron Towers," Vol. 16, No. 1, March 1957.

Brunner, Arnold W., and His Work, by Robert Ingersoll Aitken. American Institute of Architects Press, 1926.

"Cady, Berg & See, The Works of," by Montgomery Schuyler. *The Architectural Record,* Vol. 6, No. 4, April–June, 1897.

"Carrère & Hastings, The Works of Messrs." *The Architectural Record,* Vol. 27, No. 1, January 1910.

"Clinton & Russell, A Review of the Works of," by Russell Sturgis. *The Architectural Record,* Vol. 6, No. 4, April–June 1898.

"Cram, Goodhue & Ferguson, The Works of . . . ," by Montgomery Schuyler. *The Architectural Record,* Vol. 29, No. 1, January 1911.

"Davis, A. J., and the Gothic Revival," by Edna Donnell. *Metropolitan Museum Studies,* Vol. 5, No. 2, September 1936. (See also *Town [Ithiel] and Davis [A.J.].*)

"Delano & Aldrich," by W. L. Bottomley. *The Architectural Record,* Vol. 54, No. 1, July 1923.

"Eidlitz, Leopold, A Great American Architect," by Montgomery Schuyler. *The Architectural Record,* Vol. 24, No. 3, September 1908.

"Flagg, Ernest, The Works of," Introd. by H. W. Desmond. *The Architectural Record,* Vol. 11, No. 3, April 1902.

[———]: "Forgotten Pioneering," by Alan Burnham. (Singer Building, 561–563 Broadway, and the Singer Tower.) *The Architectural Forum,* Vol. 106, No. 4, April 1957.

Gilbert, Cass, Reminiscences and Addresses, edited by Julia Finch Gilbert. Privately printed, 1935.

"Haight, Charles C., A Review of the Work of," by Montgomery Schuyler. (GAAS,* No. 6.) *The Architectural Record,* July 1899.

"Hardenbergh, Henry Janeway, The Works of," by Montgomery Schuyler. *The Architectural Record,* Vol. 6, No. 3, January–March, 1897.

Hastings, Thomas, Architect . . . (with a Memoir by David Gray). Houghton Mifflin Company, 1933.

[Heins & Lafarge]: "The Cathedral of Saint John the Divine." *The Architectural Record,* Vol. 2, No. 1, July–September, 1892.

"Hunt, Richard Morris, A Review of the Work of," by Montgomery Schuyler. *The Architectural Record,* Vol. 5, No. 2, October–December 1895.

"———, The New York Architecture of," by Alan Burnham. *Journal of the Society of Architectural Historians,* Vol. 11, No. 2, May 1952.

[Kimball, Francis H.]: "The Works of Francis H. Kimball and Kimball & Thompson," by Montgomery Schuyler. *The Architectural Record,* Vol. 7, No. 4, April–June 1898.

[Kohn, Robert D.]: "An Interesting Skyscraper," by "M.S." *The Architectural Record,* Vol. 22, No. 5, November 1907.

Lafever, Minard, *The Architectural Instructor.* . . . G. P. Putnam & Co., 1856.

———, *The Beauties of Modern Architecture.* . . . D. Appleton & Co., 1839.

"Lawrence, James Crommelin, 1760–1804," by Betty J. Ezequelle. *The New-York Historical Society Quarterly,* Vol. 42, No. 3, July 1958.

[N. LeBrun]: "The Work of N. LeBrun & Sons," by Montgomery Schuyler. *The Architectural Record,* Vol. 27, No. 5, May 1910.

"Lienau, Detlef, An Architect of the Brown Decades," by Ellen W. Kramer. *Journal of the Society of Architectural Historians,* Vol. 14, No. 1, March 1955.

"McKim, Mead & White, The Works of," by Russell Sturgis. (GAAS, No. 1.) *The Architectural Record,* May 1895.

[———]: *A Monograph of the Work of McKim, Mead & White, 1879–1915* (4 vols.). The Architectural Book Publishing Co., 1915.

McKim, Charles Follen, The Life and Times of, by Charles Moore. Houghton Mifflin Company, 1929.

[Mangin, Joseph, and McComb, John]: "The New York City Hall — A Piece of Architectural History," by Montgomery Schuyler. *The Architectural Record,* Vol. 23, No. 5, May 1908.

"Post, George B., A Review of the Work of," by Russell Sturgis. (GAAS, No. 4.) *The Architectural Record,* June 1898.

"Potter, William A., The Work of," by Montgomery Schuyler. *The Architectural Record,* Vol. 26, No. 3, September 1909.

"Price, Bruce, A Review of the Works of," by Russell Sturgis. (GAAS, No. 5.) *The Architectural Record,* 1899.

* GAAS = Great American Architects Series.

[Rogers, Isaiah]: "The Old New York Custom House . . . ," by Montgomery Schuyler. *The Architectural Record*, Vol. 24, No. 6, December 1908.

"Thompson, Martin E. (1786–1877) — A Reconstruction of His Architectural Career . . . ," by Lawrence B. Romaine. *Bulletin of the New York Public Library*, Vol. 66, No. 5, May 1962.

Town [Ithiel] and Davis [A.J.], Architects, Pioneers in American Revivalist Architecture, 1817–1870, by Roger Hale Newton. Columbia University Press, 1942.

Upjohn, Richard, Architect and Churchman, by Everard M. Upjohn. Columbia University Press, 1939.

White, Stanford, by Charles C. Baldwin. Dodd, Mead & Co., 1931.

York, Edward Palmer [York & Sawyer], *Personal Reminiscences by Philip Sawyer and Royal Cortissoz*. Privately printed, 1951.

NOTE: For some of the architects listed above and for others not listed here, consult the following: Architecture–General (this Bibliography) — sources listed; *Architectural Index, The*, compiled and edited by Ervin J. Bell, Sausalito, California; *Art Index, The*, published by H. W. Wilson Co., New York City; Avery Memorial Architectural Library, Columbia University, New York City — main card index and periodical index; *Dictionary of American Biography*, Index to Vols. I–X, p. 363, 1937; Supplement I, 1944; and Supplement II, 1958, Charles Scribner's Sons; Dubois, Alfred (Elie Brault), *Les Architectes par Leurs Oeuvres* (3 vols.), H. Laurens, 1893; Withey, H. F. and E. R., *Biographical Dictionary of American Architects Deceased*, New Age Publishing Co., 1956.

BACKGROUND

Andrews, Wayne, *The Vanderbilt Legend*. . . . Harcourt, Brace & Co., Inc., 1941.

Arent, Arthur, *One-Third of a Nation*, in *Federal Theatre Plays*. Random House, 1938.

Berger, Meyer, "About New York." *New York Times*, 1953 — .(Newpaper articles.)

Botkin, B. A., editor, *New York City Folklore*. . . . Random House, 1956.

Bremer, Frederika, *Homes of the New World — Impressions of America* (2 vols.). Harper & Brothers, 1854.

Crockett Albert Stevens, *Peacocks on Parade — Life in New York 1890–1914*. Sears Publishing Co., 1931.

De Forest, Robert W., and Veiller, Lawrence, *The Tenement House Problem* (2 vols.). The Macmillan Company, 1903.

Depew, Chauncey, *My Memories of Eighty Years*. Charles Scribner's Sons, 1922.

Dickens, Charles, *American Notes* (esp. Chapter 6, "New York"). J. B. Lippincott & Co., 1885.

Ellet, (Mrs.) Elizabeth F., *The Queens of American Society*. C. Scribner & Company, 1867.

Fairfield, Francis Cary, *Clubs of New York*. H. L. Hinton, 1873.

Ford, James (with the collaboration of Katherine Morrow and George N. Thompson), *Slums and Housing with Special Reference to New York City . . .* (2 vols.). Harvard University Press, 1930.

Hamm, Margherita A., *Famous Families of New York* (2 vols.). G. P. Putnam's Sons, 1902.

Harrison, Mrs. Burton, *Recollections Grave and Gay*. Charles Scribner's Sons, 1912.

Haswell, Charles H., *Reminiscences of New York by an Octogenarian, 1816–1860*. Harper & Brothers, 1896.

Havens, Catherine E., *Diary of a Little Girl in Old New York*. Henry Collins Brown, 1920.

Hemstreet, Charles, *Nooks and Corners of Old New York*. Charles Scribner's Sons, 1899.

Henderson, Helen W., *A Loiterer in New York*. George H. Doran Co., 1917.

Howells, William Dean, *A Hazard of New Fortunes*. Harper & Brothers, 1890.

James, Henry, *Autobiography* — including *A Small Boy and Others: Notes of a Son and Brother:* and *The Middle Years* (edited with an introduction by Frederick W. Dupee). Criterion Books, Inc., 1956.

King, Moses, *Notable New Yorkers of 1896–1899*. Moses King, 1899.

Lanier, Henry Wysham, *A Century of Banking in New York, 1822–1922* (The Farmers' Loan and Trust Company Edition). The Gilliss Press, 1922.

Levy, Florence N., *A Guide to the Works of Art in New York City*. Florence N. Levy, 1916.

———, *Art in New York — A Guide to Things Worth Seeing*. The Municipal Art Society, 1939. (Index of artists, including architects.)

Lynes, Russell, *The Tastemakers*. Harper & Brothers, 1954.

McAllister, Ward, *Society As I Have Found It*. Cassell Publishing Co., 1890.

McCullough, Esther M., *As I Pass, O Manhattan*. Coley Taylor, Inc., 1956. (New York in literature.)

Martin, Edward S., *The Wayfarer in New York*. The Macmillan Company, 1909. (New York in literature.)

Meyer Berger's New York. Random House, 1960.

Mines, John Flavel, *A Tour Around New York and My Summer Acre, Being the Recollections of Mr. Felix Oldboy*. Harper & Brothers, 1893.

Monaghan, Frank, *French Travellers in the United States, 1765–1932: A Bibliography*. New York Public Library, 1933.

Morris, Lloyd, *Incredible New York*. Random House, 1951.

Myers, Gustavus, *History of Tammany Hall*. Boni & Liveright, 1917.

Nevins, Allan, editor, *America Through British Eyes*. Oxford University Press, 1923 (1948).

———, editor, *The Diary of Philip Hone, 1828–1851*. Dodd, Mead & Co., 1936.

——— and Thomas, M. H., editors, *The Diary of George Templeton Strong, 1835–1875* (4 vols.). The Macmillan Company, 1952.

Ober, C. F., and Westover, C. M., *Manhattan, Historic and Artistic — A Six Day Tour of New York City*. Lovell, Coryell & Co., 1892.

Porter, William S. (O. Henry, pseud.), *The Four Million*. Doubleday, Page & Co., 1909.

Pyne, Percy R., II, *Collection of — A Catalogue Engraved Views, Plans etc. of New York City*. Privately printed, 1912.

Rexford, Frank A., editor, *Our City — New York; A Textbook in City Government by the High School Students of New York City*. Allyn & Bacon, 1924 (1930).

Scoville, Joseph A. (Walter Barrett, pseud.), *The Old Merchants of New York City* (5 vols.). John W. Lovell Co., 1862.

Singleton, Esther, *Dutch New York*. Dodd, Mead & Co., 1909.

Still, Bayrd, *Mirror for Gotham*. New York University Press, 1956. (Foreign impressions of U.S.A.)

Tully, Andrew, *Era of Elegance*. Funk & Wagnalls Co., Inc., 1947.

Van Dyck, John G., *The New New York — A Commentary on the Place and the People* (esp. Chapter XXI, "Municipal Art"). The Macmillan Company, 1909.

Van Wyck, Frederick, *Recollections of an Old New Yorker*. Liveright Publishing Corporation, 1932.

Veblen, Thorstein, *The Theory of the Leisure Class*. The Macmillan Company, 1899.

Wecter, Dixon, *The Saga of American Society — A Record of Social Aspiration, 1607–1937*. Charles Scribner's Sons, 1937.

Weitenkampf, Frank, *The Eno Collection of New York City Views*. New York Public Library, 1925.

Wharton, Edith, *The Age of Innocence*. Grosset & Dunlap, 1920.

———, *A Backward Glance*. D. Appleton-Century Co., Inc., 1934.

————,*The House of Mirth.* Charles Scribner's Sons, 1905.

Wilson, Rufus R., and Brickson, Otilie, *New York in Literature; The Story of Landmarks of Town and Country.* Primavera Press, 1947.

CHURCHES

Anstice, Henry, *History of Saint George's Church.* Harper & Brothers, 1911.

Anthon, Henry, *Saint Mark's in the Bowery* (Parish Annals) *A Sermon Giving Historical Notices.* Stanford & Swords, 1845.

Architectural and Decorative Features of Saint Bartholomew's Church in the City of New York. Wickersham Press, Inc., 1941.

Austin, Henry, *New York and Brooklyn Churches.* Nelson & Phillips, 1874.

Berrian, William, *An Historical Sketch of Trinity Church, New York.* Stanford & Swords, 1847.

Borchers, Perry E., *Saint Paul's Chapel Recorded,* "American Notes," Charles E. Peterson, Editor. *Journal of the Society of Architectural Historians,* Vol. 19, No. 1, March 1960.

Brown, Roscoe C. E., *Church of the Holy Trinity — Brooklyn Heights. . . .* The Dunlap Press, Inc., 1922.

Brückbauer, Frederick, *The Kirk on Rutger's Farm.* Fleming H. Revell Co., 1919. (Church of the Sea and Land.)

Brumbaugh, C. E. B., "Some New York Churches During the Revolution." *American Monthly Magazine,* Vol. 40, January 1912.

Brunner, Arnold W., "Synagogue Architecture." *The Brickbuilder,* Vol. 16, No. 2, February 1907, and Vol. 16, No. 3, March 1907.

Corwin, Edward T., *A Manual of the Reformed Church in America.* Board of Publication of the Reformed Church in America, 1902.

Davies, William G., *Historical Sketch of Christ Church in New York City.* J. J. Little & Co., 1893.

DeMille, George E., *Saint Thomas Church.* Church Historical Society, 1958.

DeWitt, Thomas, *A Discourse Delivered in the North Reformed Dutch Church in the City of New York. . . .* Published by request of the Consistory, 1857.

Disosway, Gabriel P., *The Earliest Churches of New York and Its Vicinity.* James C. Gregory, 1865.

Dix, Morgan, *A History of the Parish of Trinity Church in the City of New York* (4 vols.). G. P. Putnam's Sons, 1898–1906.

Embury, Aymar, II, "Early American Churches: Part IX, Saint Paul's, Saint Mark's, Saint John's Chapel, City of New York. . . ." *The Architectural Record,* Vol. 32, No. 2, August 1912.

Farley, John M., *History of Saint Patrick's Cathedral, New York.* Society for the Propagation of the Faith, 1908.

Greenleaf, Jonathan, *A History of the Churches of All Denominations in the City of New York. . . .* E. French, 1846.

Gumaer, A. H., "The New Lady Chapel at Saint Patrick's Cathedral, New York." *The Architectural Record,* Vol. 21, No. 6, June 1907.

Hall, Edward H., *The First Presbyterian Church of New York.* American Scenic and Historic Preservation Society, 1917.

————, *A Guide to the Cathedral Church of Saint John the Divine.* Laymans Clubs of the Cathedral, 1928.

Historical Sketch of the South Church (Reformed) of New York City. Gilliss Brothers & Turnure, The Art Age Press, 1887.

Jessup, Henry W., *History of the Fifth Avenue Presbyterian Church . . . From 1808 to 1908.* . . . Fifth Avenue Presbyterian Church, 1909.

King's Handbook of New York City — Shrines of Worship, Cathedrals, Churches, Synagogues and Other Places of Religious Worship and Work. Moses King, 1893.

Memorial of Saint Mark's Church in the Bowery. . . . Published by The Vestry, 1899.

Mines, John Flavel (Felix Oldboy, pseud.), *Walks in Our Churchyards, Trinity Parish.* George Gottsberger Peck, 1903.

Onderdonk, Henry M., *History of the Protestant Episcopal Churches in the City of New-York.* Onderdonk & Gimbrede, 1843.

Patterson, Samuel White, *Old Chelsea and Saint Peter's Church.* The Friebele Press, 1935.

Perkins, J. Newton, *History of the Parish of the Incarnation, New York City 1852–1912.* "Published by the Senior Warden," 1912.

Peters, Punnett, editor, *Annals of Saint Michaels (P.E.) Church . . . for One Hundred Years 1807–1907.* G. P. Putnam's Sons, 1907.

Pratt, Helen Marshall, "Gothic Churches in New York City." *The Churchman,* Vol. 112, No. 19, November 6, 1915, and Vol. 112, No. 21, November 20, 1915.

[The Riverside Church]: *A Handbook of the Institution and Its Building.* The Riverside Church, 1931.

Ross, Ishbel, *Through the Lich Gate — A Biography of the Little Church Around the Corner.* William Farquhar Payson, 1931. (Church of the Transfiguration.)

Ryan, Leo R., *Old Saint Peter's, the Mother Church of Catholic New York, 1785–1935.* U.S. Catholic Historical Society, 1935.

Saint Patrick's Cathedral — New York. Published by the Archbishopric of New York, 1942.

Schuyler, Montgomery, "Recent Church Building in New York." *The Architectural Record,* Vol. 13, No. 6, June 1903.

———, "Italian Gothic in New York." *The Architectural Record,* Vol. 26, No. 1, July 1909.

———, "The New Saint Thomas' Church, New York." *Scribner's Magazine,* Vol. 54, No. 6, December 1913.

———, "Trinity's Architecture." *The Architectural Record,* Vol. 25, No. 6, June 1909.

The Services in Celebration of the Two-Hundredth Anniversary of the Founding of the Old First Presbyterian Church. . . . Published in the Church, Fifth Ave., Eleventh to Twelfth Streets, 1916.

Shea, John D. G., editor, *The Catholic Churches of New York City.* L. G. Goulding & Co., 1878.

Shinn, George Wolfe, *King's Handbook of Notable Episcopal Churches in the United States.* Moses King Corp'n., 1889.

Smith, John T., *The Catholic Church in New York — A History of the New York Diocese, 1808 to the Present* (2 vols.). Hall & Locke Co., 1905.

Stewart, William Rhinelander, *Grace Church and Old New York.* E. P. Dutton & Co., Inc., 1924. (Bibliography.)

Streeter, Lewis R., *Past and Present of the John Street (M. E.) Church.* Published by the author, 1913.

Titherington, Richard, "Episcopal Churches in New York." *Munsey's Magazine,* Vol. 6, No. 5, February 1892.

Wilson, James Grant, editor, *Memorial History of the City of New-York . . . ,* Vol. IV, Chapter VI, "History of Trinity Parish," by Morgan Dix; Chapter XXII, "Episcopal and Other Churches — The Protestant Episcopal Church," by Henry C. Potter, "The Catholic Church in New-York," by Richard H. Clarke. New York History Co., 1892.

Wingate, Charles F., "Saint Paul's Chapel in New York City." *American Scenic and Historic Preservation Society Reports,* Vol. 22, 1917.

Wischnitzer, Rachel, *Synagogue Architecture in the United States — History and Interpretation*. The Jewish Publication Society of America, 1955.

NOTE: For further information, consult the following magazines and the sources listed under "Architecture — General": *Church Life; The Churchman; The Ecclesiologist; Liturgical Arts.*

MONOGRAPHS OF BUILDINGS

The Appellate Division of the Supreme Court of the State of New York, First Department. The Municipal Art Society, 1957.

Boyd, John Taylor, Jr., "The Addition to the New York Harvard Club. . . ." *The Architectural Record*, Vol. 38, No. 6, December 1915.

Carstensen, George, and Gildemeister, Charles, *New York Crystal Palace Illustrated*. Riker, Thorne & Co., 1854.

Chamberlain, Samuel, editor, *Rockefeller Center — A Photographic Narrative*. Hastings House, 1947.

David, Arthur D., "The Saint Regis — The Best Type of Metropolitan Hotel." *The Architectural Record*, Vol. 15, No. 6, June 1904.

Frohne, H. W., "Designing A Metropolitan Hotel, The Plaza." *The Architectural Record*, Vol. 22, No. 5, November 1907.

Haddon, Rawson Woodman, "The Roger Morris House, New York City." Part I, *The Architectural Record*, Vol. 42, No. 1, July 1917; Part II, *ibid.*, Vol. 42, No. 11, August 1917. (Jumel Mansion.)

Hoak, E. W., and Church, W. H., *Masterpieces of Architecture in the United States*. Charles Scribner's Sons, 1930. (For the following New York buildings: Church of Saint Vincent Ferrer; Shelton Hotel; Barclay-Vesey Building; Bush Building; Woolworth Building.)

Howe, Winifred E., *A History of the Metropolitan Museum of Art*. Gilliss Press, 1913.

Hungerford, Edward, *The Story of the Waldorf-Astoria*. G. P. Putnam's Sons, 1925.

The Last Rivet — The Story of Rockefeller Center — A City Within A City. . . . Columbia University Press, 1940.

Levine, Benjamin, and Story, Isabelle F., *Statue of Liberty, National Monument, Bedloe's Island, New York*. National Park Service Historical Handbook Series, No. 11, 1952.

Marshall, David, *Grand Central*. Whittlesey House, McGraw-Hill Book Co., Inc., 1946.

"National Maine Monument Competition." *The Architectural Annual*, Architectural League of America (Albert W. Kelsey, editor), issue for 1901.

Peyser, Ethel R., *The House That Music Built — The Story of Carnegie Hall*. Robert M. McBride & Co., 1936.

Price, C. Matlack, and Hunter, George L., "The Avery Library." *The Architectural Record*, Vol. 33, No. 6, June 1913. (Columbia University.)

Reed, Henry Hope, Jr., *The City Hall of the City of New York*. Issued by The Municipal Art Society in honor of The National Trust for Historic Preservation, 1961.

Schuyler, Montgomery, "The New Custom House at New York." *The Architectural Record*, Vol. 20, No. 1, July 1906.

——, "New York City Hall. . . ." *The Architectural Record*, Vol. 23, No. 5, May 1908.

——, "The New York Stock Exchange." *The Architectural Record*, Vol. 12, No. 4, September 1902.

——, "The Old New York Custom House and the New City Bank." *The Architectural Record*, Vol. 24, No. 6, December 1908. (First National City Bank of New York.)

——, "The Restoration of Fraunces Tavern." *The Architectural Record*, Vol. 24, No. 6, December 1908.

——, *The Woolworth Building*. Privately printed by the Munder-Thomsen Co., 1913.

Semsch, O. F., *A History of the Singer Building Construction — Its Progress from Foundation to Flag Pole.* Shumway & Beattie, 1908.

Shear, John Knox, editor, "One Hundred Years of Significant Building" *The Architectural Record,* as follows: Rockefeller Center, p. 150, June 1956; The Villard Mansion, p. 192, October 1956; The University Club, p. 225, March 1957.

Shelton, William H., *Jumel Mansion — Being a History of the House on Harlem Heights.* . . . Houghton Mifflin Company, 1916.

Starrett, W. A., *Empire State: A Pictorial Record of Its Construction.* William Edwin Rudge, 1931.

Steinman, David B., *The Builders of the Bridge — The Story of John Roebling and His Son.* Hartcourt, Brace & Co., Inc., 1945. (Bibliography.) (Brooklyn Bridge.)

Stewart, William Rhinelander, *The Washington Arch in Washington Square.* Ford & Garnett, 1895.

Sturgis, Russell, "Façade of the New York Stock Exchange." *The Architectural Record,* Vol. 16, No. 5, November 1904.

Torres, Louis, "Samuel Thomson and the Old Custom House." *Journal of the Society of Architectural Historians,* Vol. 20, No. 4, December 1961. (Federal Hall National Memorial, former United States Subtreasury.)

Van Pelt, John Vredenburgh, *A Monograph of the W. K. Vanderbilt House — Richard Morris Hunt, Architect.* John Vredenburgh Van Pelt, 1925.

Weisman, Winston, "Who Designed Rockefeller Center?" *Journal of the Society of Architectectural Historians,* Vol. 10, No. 1, March 1951.

PARKS AND SQUARES

Andrews, William Loring, *The Iconography of the Battery and Castle Garden.* Charles Scribner's Sons, 1901.

Central Park Association, *The Central Park.* Thomas Seltzer, 1926.

Foord, John, *The Life and Public Services of Andrew Haswell Green.* Doubleday, Page & Co., 1913. (Central Park.)

Gilder, Rodman, *The Battery.* . . . Houghton Mifflin Company, 1936.

Halper, Albert, *Union Square.* The Viking Press, Inc., 1933.

A Handbook for Prospect Park, Brooklyn, L.I. . . . E. B. Tripp, 1874.

Historical Sketch of Madison Square. Meriden, Britannia Co., n.d.

James, Henry, *Washington Square.* Harper & Brothers, 1881.

Nadal, E. S., "New Parks of the City of New York. *Scribner's Magazine,* Vol. 11, No. 4, April 1892.

Olmsted, Frederick Law, Jr., and Kimball, Theodora, editors. *Frederick Law Olmsted, Landscape Architect, 1822–1903;* Vol. II, *Central Park.* G. P. Putnam's Sons, 1928.

Parsons, Mabel, editor, *Memories of Samuel Parsons, Landscape Architect of the Department of Public Parks, New York.* G. P. Putnam's Sons, 1926.

Pine, John B., *The Story of Gramercy Park, 1831–1921.* Reprinted by permission from *Valentine's Manual* and published with additions by the Gramercy Park Association, 1921.

Platt, Raye R., editor, *New York Walk Book* (American Geographical Society Outing Series No. 2). American Geographical Society, 1923.

Richards, T. Addison, *Guide to The Central Park.* James Miller, 1866.

Schuyler, Montgomery, "New York's City Hall Park Problem." *Outlook,* Vol. 95, July 23, 1910.

Stoddard, J. L., *Famous Parks and Public Buildings of America.* The Werner Co., 1899.

NOTE: See also *The Green,* Vol. 1, No. 1, 1958, published by the Park Association of New York City, 15 Gramercy Park, New York 3, N.Y.

RESIDENCES

Bank of the Manhattan Company, *Historic Buildings Now Standing in New York Which Were Erected Prior to Eighteen Hundred.* Printed for Bank of the Manhattan Company, 1914. (Residences in Greater New York.)

Berton, G., "Hamilton Grange Today." *Mentor*, Vol. 17, July 1939.

Browne, Junius Henri, "The Problem of Living in New York." *Harper's New Monthly Magazine*, Vol. 65, No. 390, November 1882.

Colt, H. Dunscombe, *Hidden Houses of New York.* The Two Horse Press, 1960.

Croly, Herbert, "The Contemporary New York Residence." *The Architectural Record*, Vol. 12, No. 7, December 1902.

————, "Renovation of the Brownstone District." *The Architectural Record*, Vol. 13, No. 6, June 1903.

Dean, Bashford, and Welch, McMillan, *The Dyckman House.* Annual Report of the American Scenic & Historic Preservation Society. J. B. Tryon Co., 1917.

DeForest, Robert W., and Veiller, Lawrence, *The Tenement House Problem* (2 vols.). The Macmillan Company, 1903.

"A Fifth Avenue Mansion." *The Architectural Record*, Vol. 27, No. 5, May 1910. (Residence of Edward S. Harkness.)

"Great American Residences" series, "Residence of Andrew Carnegie." *The Architectural Record*, Vol. 13, No. 1, January 1903.

Lamb, Charles R., *The Tilden Mansion.* The National Arts Club, 1932.

"A New Type of City House." *The Architectural Record*, Vol. 22, No. 3, September 1907. (Residence of Ernest Flagg.)

Pelletreau, William S. *Early New York Houses with Historical and Genealogical Notes. . . .* Francis P. Harper, 1900.

Riis, Jacob, *How the Other Half Lives — Studies Among the Tenements of New York.* Charles Scribner's Sons, 1890.

Schuyler, Montgomery (signed "M.S."), "Dwellings." Part III, *The American Architect & Building News*, Vol. 9, No. 278, April 23, 1881; Part IV, *ibid.*, Vol. 9, No. 279, April 30, 1881; Part V, "The Vanderbilt Houses," *ibid.*, Vol. 9, No. 282, May 21, 1881.

————, "The New York House." *The Architectural Record*, Vol. 19, No. 2, February 1906.

————, "The Small City House in New York." *The Architectural Record*, Vol. 8, No. 4, April–June 1899.

————, (Franz Winkler, pseud.), "Architecture in the Billionaire District of New York City." *The Architectural Record*, Vol. 11, No. 2, October 1901.

Shaw, C. G., "A Metropolitan Antique." *Antiques*, Vol. 45, No. 4, April 1944. (Smith's Folly — Abigail Adams Smith House.)

Solon, Leon V., "The Residence of Otto H. Kahn, Esq., New York. . . ." *The Architectural Record*, Vol. 46, No. 11, August 1919.

Stapley, Mildred, "The Last Dutch Farmhouses in New York City." *The Architectural Record*, Vol. 32, No. 1, July 1912.

Sturgis, Russell, "The Art Gallery of the New York Streets." *The Architectural Record*, Vol. 10, No. 1, July 1900.

————, John W. Root, Bruce Price, and others, *The City House in the East and South — Homes in City and Country.* Charles Scribner's Sons, 1893.

Tuthill, William Burnet, *The City Residence, Its Design and Construction.* William T. Comstock, 1890.

Van Rensselaer, Marianna G., "Recent Architecture in America." "City Dwellings — I," *Century Magazine*, Vol. 31, No. 4, February 1886; "City Dwellings — II," *ibid.*, Vol. 31, No. 5, March 1886.

White, Richard Grant, "Old New York and its Houses." *Century Magazine,* Vol. 26, No. 6, October 1883.

NOTE: See also "Architecture — General" and "Architects" in this bibliography.

SCULPTURE

Adams, A., "A Family of Sculptors." *American Magazine of Art,* Vol. 12, No. 7, July 1921. (The Piccirillis.)

The Art Commission of the City of New York, *Catalogue of the Works of Art Belonging to the City of New York — Sculpture.* Published by the Commission: Vol. I, 1909; Vol. II, 1920.

Barker, Albert W., "Louis H. Sullivan, Thinker and Architect." *The Architectural Annual,* Architectural League of America (Albert W. Kelsey, editor), issue of 1901.

Bartlett, E. S., "Paul Bartlett: American Sculptor." *New England Magazine,* Vol. 33, No. 4, December 1905.

Byne, Arthur G., "The Salient Characteristics of the Work of Charles Keck." *The Architectural Record,* Vol. 32, No. 2, August 1912.

Caffin, Charles H., *American Masters of Sculpture.* . . . Doubleday, Page & Co., 1903.

Clark, William J. Jr., *Great American Sculptures.* Gebbie & Barrie, 1878.

Cortissoz, Royal, "An American Sculptor." *The Studio,* Vol. 6, No. 32, October 1895. (MacMonnies.)

————, *Augustus Saint-Gaudens.* Houghton Mifflin Company, 1907.

Dennis, L. C., "A Great American Sculptor." *Review of Reviews,* Vol. 19, No. 1, January 1899. (G. G. Barnard.)

Dorr, Charles H., "A Sculptor of Monumental Architecture." *The Architectural Record,* Vol. 33, No. 6, June 1913. (A. A. Weinman.)

Gallatin, A. E., *Paul Manship.* John Lane Company, 1917.

Gardner, Albert Ten Eyck, *Yankee Stonecutters, The First American School of Sculpture 1800–1850.* Published for the Metropolitan Museum of Art by Columbia University Press, 1945. (Including: "Precursors"; "A Biographical Dictionary"; "The Successors"; and a bibliography.)

Hartmann, Sadakichi, editor, *Modern American Sculpture.* . . . Paul Wenzel, 1918.

Henderson, Helen W., *A Loiterer in New York.* George H. Doran Co., 1917.

Holden, J. S., "Sculptors MacNeil." *World's Work,* Vol. 14, No. 6, October 1906.

King, Moses, editor. *King's Handbook of New York City — Thoroughfares and Adornments, Monuments, Statues, Fountains.* . . . Moses King, 1893.

Levy, Florence N., editor, *A Guide to the Works of Art in New York City.* Florence N. Levy, 1916.

National Sculpture Society, *Catalogue of Exhibition of American Sculpture, New York, April 14 to August 1, 1923.* (Includes biographies of the sculptors.)

Payne, Frank Owen, "Notable Decorative Sculptures of New York Buildings." *The Architectural Record,* Vol. 47, No. 2, February 1902.

Peixotto, E., "Sculpture of Herbert Adams." *American Magazine of Art,* Vol. 12, 1921.

Poore, H. R., "Stirling Calder, Sculptor." *International Studio,* Vol. 67, No. 267, April 1919.

Saint-Gaudens, Homer, editor, *The Reminiscences of Augustus Saint-Gaudens* (2 vols.). The Century Company, 1913.

Saltus, J. Sanford, and Tisné, Walter E., *Statues of New York.* G. P. Putnam's Sons, 1923.

Schaub-Koch, E., *Anna Hyatt-Huntington.* . . . Hispanic Society of America, 1936.

Schevill, Ferdinand, *Karl Bitter.* University of Chicago Press, 1917.

Sturgis, Russell, "The Work of J. Q. A. Ward." *Scribner's Magazine,* Vol. 32, No. 4, October 1902.

Tachau, H., "Lee Lawrie, Architectural Sculptor." *International Studio*, Vol. 75, No. 303, August 1922.

Taft, Lorado, "Daniel Chester French, Sculptor." *Brush and Pencil*, Vol. 5, No. 4, January 1900.

———, *The History of American Sculpture*. The Macmillan Company, 1930. (Bibliography.)

Wilson, James Grant, editor, *Memorial History of the City of New-York . . .* , Vol. IV, Chapter VII, "The Statues and Monuments of New-York," by Walter S. Wilson. New York History Co., 1892.

NOTE: Consult also the following for further information: *American Magazine of Art;* Architectural League catalogues; *The Architectural Record; Art World; The Craftsman; International Studio; Monumental News; National Sculpture Review;* National Sculpture Society, 1083 Fifth Avenue, New York City; New York City Department of Parks and Monuments, Monument Restoration Division, The Arsenal, Central Park at 64th Street, New York City.

STREETS AND AVENUES

Brierly, J. Ernest, *The Streets of Old New York*. Hastings House, 1953.

Brown, Henry Collins, *Fifth Avenue, Old and New, 1824–1924*. Official publication of The Fifth Avenue Association, 1924.

Collins, Francis A., *The Romance of Park Avenue*. The Park Avenue Association, Inc., 1930.

Comstock, Sarah, *Old Roads From the Heart of New York . . . Within Thirty Miles Around the Battery*. G. P. Putnam's Sons, 1915.

Davis, Richard Harding, "Broadway." In *The Great Streets of the World*. Charles Scribner's Sons, 1892.

De Leeuw, R. M., *Up Both Sides of Broadway*. The De Leeuw, Riehl Publishing Co., 1910.

Dunshee, Kenneth H., *As You Pass By*. Hastings House, 1952. ("A Directory of Forgotten Streets," following p. 270, relates former street names to those of today.)

Fifth Avenue Association, *Fifty Years on Fifth, 1907–1957*. The Fifth Avenue Association, 1957. (Bibliography.)

Fifth Avenue Events. Fifth Avenue Bank of New York, 1916.

Fifth Avenue — Glances at the Vicissitudes and Romance of a World Renowned Thoroughfare. . . . Printed for the Fifth Avenue Bank of New York, 1915.

Gerard, James W., *Old Dutch Streets of New York, Under the Dutch*. D. Taylor, 1874.

Haddon, Rawson Woodman, "Varick Street Which Is in Greenwich Village, Manhattan." *The Architectural Record*, Vol. 35, No. 1, January 1914.

Harlow, Alvin, *Old Bowery Days: The Chronicles of a Famous Street*. D. Appleton & Co., 1931.

Hill, Frederick Trevor, *Story of a Street: The Narrative History of Wall Street from 1644–1908*. Harper & Brothers, 1908.

Hyde, E. Belcher, *Miniature Atlas — Borough of Manhattan in One Volume*. E. Belcher Hyde, 1912.

Jenkins, Stephen, *The Greatest Street in the World — The Story of Broadway. . . .* G. P. Putnam's Sons, 1911.

Lamb, M. S., *Wall Street in History*. Funk & Wagnalls Co., 1883.

Levinson, Leonard L., *Wall Street — A Pictorial History*. A. S. Barnes & Company, Inc., 1962.

McKay, Richard C., *South Street: A Maritime History of New York*. G. P. Putnam's Sons, 1934.

Manchester, Herbert, *Lower Broadway and the Fulton Trust Company of New York, 1890–1930*. Fulton Trust Company of New York, 1930.

Maurice, Arthur Bartlett, *Fifth Avenue*. Dodd, Mead & Co., 1918.

Osborn, Gardner, *Streets of Old New York*. Harper & Brothers, 1939.

Perine, E. T. B., *Here's to Broadway*. G. P. Putnam's Sons, 1930.

Post, John J., *Old Streets, Roads, Lanes, Piers and Wharves of New York*. R. D. Cooke, 1882.

Pratt, Sereno S., *Work of Wall Street*. D. Appleton & Co., 1904.

Reeves, William Fullerton, *The First Elevated Railroads on Manhattan and the Bronx of the City of New York. . . .* (Vol. IX of the John Divine Jones Fund Series.) New-York Historical Society, 1936.

Ruhl, Arthur, "Building New York's Subway." *Century Magazine*, Vol. LXIV (Vol. 42 New Series), No. 6, October 1902.

Schoonmaker, F. W., *Yesterday and Today on Forty-Second-Street*. Press of the Chauncey Holt Co., 1926.

True, Clarence, *Riverside Drive*. Press of Unz & Co., 1899.

Twenty-third Street Association, Inc., Twenty-fifth Anniversary 1929–1954. Twenty-third Street Association, 1954.

Wakeman, Abram, *History of Lower Wall Street*. The Spice Mill Publishing Co., 1914.

Walton, Frank, *Tomahawks to Textiles — The Fabulous Story of Worth Street*. Appleton-Century-Crofts, Inc., 1953.

PRESERVATION OF BUILDINGS — U.S.A.

Allison, David, "Mapping and Measuring in 3-D." *Architectural Forum*, Vol. 108, No. 6, June 1958. (Photogrammetry.)

American Institute of Architects, Committee for the Preservation of Historic Buildings, *Arousing the Community to Its Architectural Heritage*. The Institute, 1961.

Appleton, William Sumner, "Destruction and Preservation of Old New England Buildings." *Art & Archaeology*, Vol. 8, No. 3, May–June 1919.

Architectural Forum, editors, *Architecture Worth Saving*. Catalogue for exhibit at the Museum of Modern Art, reprinted from the *Architectural Forum*, June 1958. (See also Vol. 108, No. 6, June 1958.)

Architectural Forum, "An Instinct for Preservation." Editorial, Vol. 118, No. 3, March 1963.

————, "The Value of Used Architecture." Editorial, Vol. 106, No. 4, April 1957.

Bard, Albert S., "Aesthetics and the Police Power." *American Journal of Economics and Sociology*, Vol. 15, No. 3, 1956.

————, "The Municipal Regulation of Esthetics Advanced." *The American City*, Vol. 71, No. 9, September 1956.

Barrington, Lewis, *Historic Restorations of the Daughters of the American Revolution*. Richard R. Smith, 1941.

Borchers, Perry E., "Saint Paul's Chapel Recorded" (by photogrammetry). In "American Notes," Charles E. Peterson, editor, *Journal of the Society of Architectural Historians*, Vol. 19, No. 1, March 1960.

Brown, G. Baldwin, *The Care of Ancient Monuments*. Cambridge University Press, 1905. See esp. Appendix, "The Care of Monuments in the United States of America."

Bullock, Helen Duprey, "What is A Shrine?" Editorial, *Historic Preservation*, Vol. 9, No. 2, 1956.

Burr, R. Nelson, compiler, *Safeguarding Our Cultural Heritage: A Bibliography on the Protection of Museums, Works of Art, Monuments . . . in Time of War*. Library of Congress, General Reference and Bibliography Division, 1952.

Carver, John A., Jr., "An Inexact Business." *American Institute of Architects Journal*, Vol. 39, No. 2, February 1963.

Clark, Blake, "Wanton Disregard of Our Heritage." *Reader's Digest,* Vol. 74, No. 441, January 1959.

Codman, John, *Preservation of Historic Districts by Architectural Control.* American Society of Planning Officials, 1956.

Coleman, Laurence Vail, *Historic House Museums.* The American Association of Museums, 1933. (A directory with bibliography.)

Coolidge, John, "William Morris on the Preservation of Historic Monuments." *Journal of the American Society of Architectural Historians,* Vol. 4, No. 2, April 1944.

Dunbar, Philip H., "Don't Tear That Old House Down." *The Journal of Long Island History,* Vol. 2, No. 2, Fall 1962.

Fagin, Henry, and Weinberg, Robert C., editors, *Planning and Community Appearance.* Regional Plan Association, 1958. (Bibliography — "A Selected List of References on Planning for Community Appearance.")

Feiss, Carl, *Community Architecture: An Appeal to Action.* The American Institute of Architects, 1962. (Bibliography.)

Gilman, B. I., "Museums of Art and the Conservation of Monuments." *Proceedings,* American Association of Museums, Vol. 3, May 11, 1913.

Harper, Mr. (pseudonym), "After Hours — To the Barricades." *Harper's Magazine,* Vol. 210, No. 1256, January 1955.

Historic American Buildings Survey, *Catalogue of Measured Drawings and Photographs. . . .* National Park Service, Department of the Interior, 1941; Supplement, January 1959.

Historic Preservation, Vol. 13, No. 4, 1961. This number is devoted to a review of preservation activity in cities throughout the nation.

"Historic Preservation Via Urban Renewal." *Journal of Housing,* Issue No. 6, Volume 19, August 10, 1962.

Hosmer, Charles, *Old Homes in America . . . Preservation to 1926.* Ph.D. dissertation, unpublished, Teachers College, Columbia University, 1961. (Bibliography.)

Jacobs, Stephen W., and Jones, Barclay G., *City Design through Conservation: Methods for the Evaluation and Utilization of Aesthetics and Cultural Resources.* Unpublished study sponsored by the Rockefeller Foundation, University of California, 1960. (Bibliographical footnotes.)

Journal of the American Society of Architectural Historians, Vol. 1, Nos. 3–4, July–October 1941. (Special issue devoted to the preservation of historic monuments; articles by Hans Huth, Kenneth J. Conant, Fiske Kimball, Newton B. Drury, William Sumner Appleton, Helen G. McCormack, Charles E. Peterson, Carl Feiss, and Robert Moses; see esp. "Preservation," a selected bibliography by Hans Huth.)

Lee, Ronald F., *United States: Historical and Archaeological Monuments.* Instituto Panamericano de Geografía e Historia, Comisión de Historia, 1951.

Lockwood, Alice G. B., "Problems and Responsibilities of Restoration." *Old Time New England,* Vol. 28, No. 2, October 1937.

Morrison, Jacob H., *Historic Preservation Law.* Pelican Pub. Co., 1957. (Legal aspects of preservation giving laws and case histories.)

Moses, Robert, Commissioner, *Construction and Restoration of Monuments, Memorials and Historic Buildings . . . Manhattan, Brooklyn, Bronx, Queens and Richmond.* Department of Parks, City of New York, 1941.

Municipal Art Society of New York, *Bulletin.* No. 1, 1903; No. 25, 1905; and No. 1, 1915; No. 20, 1920. Later *Bulletins* (not numbered), 1930–1941.

National Archives, editors, *Tentative Bibliography on the Conservation of Cultural Resources in Time of War.* National Archives, 1941.

National Trust Committee on Standards and Surveys, *Criteria for Evaluating Historical Sites and Buildings.* The Committee, May 1956. (A report.)

New-York Historical Society, "Report on the Preservation of New York by a Committee of the Society's Trustees." *New-York Historical Society Bulletin*, Vol. 25, April 1941.

New York State Historical Association and the National Trust, "Primer for Preservation — A Handbook for Historic Housekeeping." *Antiques*, July 1956. (A reprint.)

"Preservation Leaflet" series, compiled by the National Trust for Historic Preservation. (Includes a bibliography on preservation, undated.)

Preservation News. Monthly newsletter, the National Trust for Historic Preservation, Vol. 1, No. 1, January 1961–

Pressey, Park, "Preserving the Landmarks." *House Beautiful,* Vol. 36, No. 4, September 1914.

The Providence City Plan Commission in Cooperation with the Providence Preservation Society and the H.H.F.A., *College Hill: A Demonstration Study of Historic Area Renewal.* The Commission, 1959.

Roehrich Pact, *The Treaty Between the United States of America and Other Republics for the Protection of Artistic and Scientific Institutions and Historic Monuments.* Government Printing Office, 1936.

Schneider, J. Thomas, *Report to the Secretary of the Interior on the Preservation of Historic Sites and Buildings.* Department of the Interior, 1935.

Schuyler, Montgomery, "On Letting It Alone." In "Notes and Comments," *The Architectural Record*, Vol. 18, No. 5, November 1905.

Sturges, W. Knight, "Architectural Preservation in New York." *Oculus* (Newsletter), Vol. 33, No. 4, January 1962.

Vrooman, John J., "Preservationism in New York State." *Journal of the American Society of Architectural Historians,* Vol. 4, No. 2, April 1944.

NOTE: See also publications of the following societies, etc.: American Institute of Architects, Committee for the Preservation of Historic Buildings, 343 So. Dearborn St., Chicago, Ill.; American Scenic and Historic Preservation Society, New York City; Committee on Preservation and Restoration of Canals and Historic Sites and Buildings, Albany, N.Y.; Municipal Art Society of New York, Committee on Historic Architecture, Committee on Landmarks; Museum of the City of New York; National Trust for Historic Preservation, Washington, D.C.; New York State Historical Association, Cooperstown, N.Y.; New-York Historical Society, New York City; Society of Architectural Historians, New York Chapter; Society for the Preservation of New England Antiquities, Boston, Mass. No attempt has been made to list in this bibliography the countless publications covering instances of actual preservation and restoration of towns and buildings.

X. INDEX OF ARCHITECTS

Including Engineers and Builders listed in "Index of Architecturally Notable Structures in Greater New York"

Goodhue, Bertram G., 359, 364, 365; *see also* Cram, Goodhue & Ferguson
Graves and Duboy, 374
Haight, Charles C., 372
Hale and Rogers, 371
Harde & Short, 375
Hardenbergh, Henry J., 362, 363, 367
Harmon, Arthur Loomis, 369
Harrison, Wallace K., *see* Corbett, Harrison and MacMurray
Hastings, Thomas, 360, 374; *see also* Carrère and Hastings
Heath, John, 366, 373
Heins and LaFarge, 358, 383
Helmle and Corbett, 370
Helmle and Huberty, 379
Hiss and Weekes, 369
Hofmeister, H., *see* Reinhard and Hofmeister
Hood, Raymond, 371, 374; *see also* Hood and Fouilhoux; Hood, Godley and Fouilhoux
Hood and Fouilhoux, 371
Hood, Godley and Fouilhoux, 370
Howells and Stokes, 373
Hubert, Pirrson & Co., 374
Huberty, *see* Helmle and Huberty
Hunt, Richard H., 360, 369
Hunt, Richard Morris, 358, 360
Hunting and Jacobsen, 367
Huntington, Charles Pratt, 373
Jackson, Thomas R., 369
Jacobsen, *see* Hunting and Jacobsen
Kellum, J. W., *see* King and Kellum
Kimball, Francis H., 380, 381
King, Gamaliel, 378; *see also* King and Kellum
King and Kellum, 365
King and Wilcox, 380
Kohn, Robert D., 370
LaFarge, C. G., *see* Heins and LaFarge
Lafever, Minard, 364, 365, 366, 372, 378, 380, 381, 383
Lake, Daniel, 388
Lawrence, James C., 357
LeBrun, N., and Sons, 363
L'Enfant, Major Pierre C., 377
Littell, Emlen T., 372
Livingston, G., *see* Trowbridge and Livingston
Lord, James Brown, 367
Lowinson, Oscar, 374
McBean, Thomas, 357
McComb, John, Jr., 357, 363; *see also* Mangin and McComb
MacDonald, Charles, engineer, 368
Mackenzie, A., *see* Eidlitz and Mackenzie
McKenzie, Voorhees and Gmelin, 374
McKenzie, Voorhees, Gmelin and Walker, 380
McKim, Mead & White, 357, 360, 361, 362, 364, 365, 366, 369, 370, 373, 375, 384

MacMurray, William H., *see* Corbett, Harrison and MacMurray
Maginnis and Walsh, 374
Magonigle, H. Van Buren, 367
Mangin, Joseph F., *see* Doyle and Mangin; Mangin and McComb
Mangin and McComb, 357
Matthews, Charles T., 359
Mayers, Murray and Phillip, 359, 364, 366
Mead, William R., *see* McKim, Mead & White
Mersereau, William H., 368, 388
Morgan, Lloyd, 363
Morris, Benjamin W., 357, 374
Morris, Montrose W., 382
Morse, George L., 380
Morton, Oliver P., 384
Mould, J. Wrey, *see* Vaux and Mould
Murray, *see* Mayers, Murray and Phillip
Olmsted, Frederick L., 368; *see also* Olmsted and Vaux; Olmsted, Vaux & Co.
Olmsted and Vaux, 360
Olmsted, Vaux & Co., 379
O'Rourke, Jeremiah, 365
Paten, David, 386
Peterson, Frederic A., 367, 378, 379
Phillip, H., *see* Mayers, Murray and Phillip
Pirrson, James W., *see* Hubert, Pirrson & Co.
Pope, John Russell, 359, 363
Pope, Theodate, 371
Post, George B., 361, 368, 375, 380
Potter, William A., 359
Price, Bruce, 374
Putnam and Cox, 384
Radford, *see* Vaux & Radford
Rainsford, Kerr, 372
Reed and Stem, 368
Reinhard and Hofmeister, 371
Renwick, James, Jr., 357, 359, 384, 387
Renwick and Sands, 379
Robertson, Robert H., 384
Roebling, John A., engineer, 360
Roebling, Washington A., engineer, 360
Rogers, Isaiah, 359, 370
Rogers, James G., *see* Hale and Rogers
Rose and Stone, 375
Russell, W. H., *see* Clinton and Russell
Saeltzer, Alexander, 367
Sands, Joseph, *see* Renwick and Sands
Sawyer, Philip, *see* York & Sawyer
Schickel & Ditmars, 364
Short, *see* Harde & Short
Smith, I. L., 383
Smith, James W., builder, 366
Smith, Lyndon P., 362
Snook, John B., 374, 375

XI. GENERAL INDEX

NOTE: *Figures in italics indicate illustrations*

Maginnis, Charles D., Sr., *see* Maginnis and
    Walsh
Maginnis and Walsh, 374
Magonigle, H. Van Buren, 252, 367
Magruder, Charles, 8
Main Post Office, Brooklyn, 318, *319*, 380
Main Street, 15, 47
Maine Memorial, 252, *253*, 367
Mall, Central Park, 22, *23*
Mangin, Joseph F., 34, 70; *see also* Doyle and
    Mangin; Mangin and McComb
Mangin and McComb, 70, 357
Manhattan Club, 39, 134, *135*, 369
Manhattan Square, 21
Manor of Bentley, 342
Mansard roof, 38, 39
Mansart, Jules H., 38
Manship, Paul, 29
Marble Collegiate Church, 40, 122, *123*, 365
Margaret Hotel, *see* Hotel Margaret
Marine Hospital, United States, 388
Mariners' Temple, 365
Markowitz, Arnold L., 8
Martiny, Philip, 366
Matthews, Charles T., 359
Mausolos, King, 166
Mayers, Francis L. S., *see* Mayers, Murray and
    Phillip
Mayers, Murray and Phillip, 359, 364, 366
Mayor of New York City, 16
Mead, William R., *see* McKim, Mead & White
Mediaevalism regenerated, 40
Meière, Hildreth, 366
Merchants' Exchange, 35, 242, 370
Merchants' Gate, 367
Merchant's House, Old, 84, *85*, 364
Merrill, Charles E., 7
Mersereau, William H., 368, 388
Metal Exchange Building, 80, *81*, 374
Metropolitan Club, 176, *177*, 362
Metropolitan Life Insurance Company
    Tower, 236, *237*, 363
Metropolitan Museum of Art, 24, 78, *79*, 194,
    195, 360, 361
Metropolitan Opera House, 368
Middle Dutch Reformed Church, 58
Miller, William Starr, residence, 50, 262,
    263, 371
Mission of Our Lady of the Rosary, *see* Our
    Lady of the Rosary, Mission of
Mission Society, New York, 174
Modified, 54
Montauk Club, 52, 320, *321*, 380
Monticello, 36
Moore, Clement C., 366
Moorish Revival style, 36, 41
Moravian Church, 388

Morgan, J. P., 176, 214
Morgan, Lloyd, 363
Morgan Guaranty Trust Company, *see*
    Guaranty Trust Building
Morgan Library, 214, *215*, 357
Morningside Park, 24
Morris, Benjamin W., 357, 374
Morris, Montrose W., 382
Morris, Roger, 56
Morris-Jumel House, 32, 56, *57*, 363
Morris Tombs, *see* St. Ann's Church, Bronx
Morse, George L., 380
Morton, Oliver P., *see* Putnam and Cox
Mott Haven Railroad Station, 384
Mould, J. Wrey, 22; *see also* Vaux and Mould
Mount Morris Park, 21; watchtower, 120, *121*
Municipal Art Society, 3–4, 7, 8, 18, 192
Municipal Building, Brooklyn, 380
Murray, *see* Mayers, Murray and Phillip
Museum of the American Indian, 373
Museum of Art, *see* Metropolitan Museum of
    Art
Museum of the City of New York, 64
Museum of Natural History, *see* American
    Museum of Natural History

Napoleon I, 41, 166
Napoleon III, 38
National Academy of Design, 44
National Arts Club, 136, *137*, 369
National City Bank, 242
National Park Bank, old, 28
National Park Service, 16, 17
National Sculpture Society, 8, 18
National Shrines Advisory Board, 18
National style, 30, 35, 42, 44, 49, 53
National Trust for Historic Preservation, 17
Natural History Museum, *see* American
    Museum of Natural History
Navy Yard Hospital Building, 286, *287*, 378
Neo-Grec style, 42–43, 132, 352
Neville house, *see* Old Stone Jug
New Haven, Connecticut, 41
New Lots Dutch Reformed Church, 379
Newman, Ben, 7
Newport, Rhode Island, 41
New Utrecht Reformed Church, 381
New York Central Building, 26
New York Chapter, *see* American Institute of
    Architects
New York City Hall, *see* City Hall, New York
New York Community Trust, 4, 6, 18
New York Cotton Exchange, 94
New York County Lawyers Association, 280,
    281, 360
New York Daily News Building, *see* Daily
    News Building

PICTURE CREDITS

NEW YORK LANDMARKS

The text of this book was set in Linotype Primer by
Connecticut Printers, Inc. The chapter headings and
other display lines were hand-set in Augustea by Phil-
mac Typographers. Both text and the photographs,
many of which were taken especially for this work,
were printed in fine-screen offset lithography by the
Meriden Gravure Company. The binding was done by
Russell-Rutter, Inc.

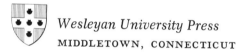 *Wesleyan University Press*
MIDDLETOWN, CONNECTICUT

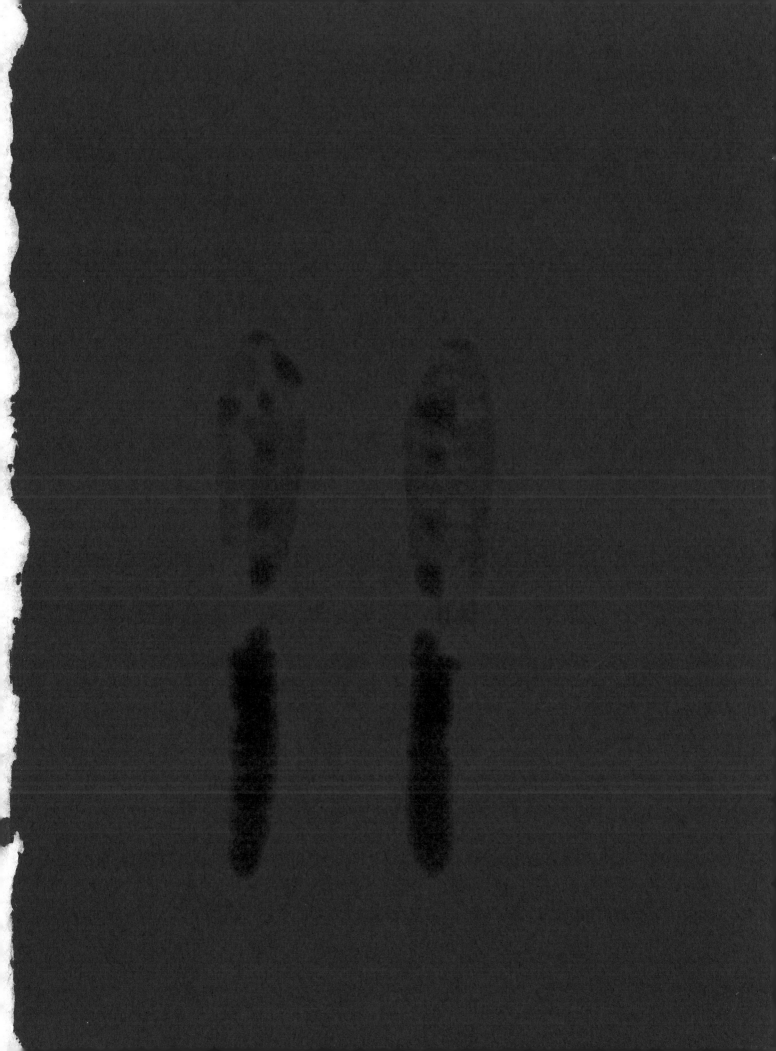